# ANSWERS
## for Today

# Volumes 1 & 2

### BY CHUCK SMITH

The Word For Today Publishers
Costa Mesa, California 92628

**Answers for Today, Volumes 1 & 2**

by Chuck Smith

© 1993 The Word For Today

Published by TWFT Publishers,
P.O. Box 8000, Costa Mesa, California 92628
(800) 272-WORD (9673)
Web site: http://www.thewordfortoday.org

ISBN 0-936728-52-3
(Previous ISBN 0-936728-43-4)

Unless otherwise indicated, Scripture quotations in this book are taken from the King James Version of the Bible. Translational emendations, amplifications, and paraphrases are by the author.

# TABLE OF CONTENTS

# CHAPTER 1

*After the long night—*

# IT'S TIME FOR THE SONRISE!

> And that, knowing the time, that now it is high time to awake out of sleep: for now is our salvation nearer than when we believed. The night is far spent, the day is at hand: let us therefore cast off the works of darkness, and let us put on the armor of light. Let us walk honestly, as in the day; not in rioting and drunkenness,...not in strife and envying: but put ye on the Lord Jesus Christ, and make not provision for the flesh, to fulfill the lusts thereof (Romans 13:11–14).

Jesus Christ never intended for His people to be taken by surprise at His coming. He intends for you to be totally aware of the time of His return, so that you would be watching, waiting, and ready when He comes again. Scriptures that refer to His coming again as "a thief in the night" do not refer to the way the church will experience His return, but to the way the world will see it. The coming of Christ will take the world totally by surprise—but not

1

the Christian. Paul said, "But ye, brethren, are not in darkness, that the day should overtake you as a thief. Ye are all the children of the light" (1 Thessalonians 5:4, 5).

"Knowing the time." The children of the light know that the coming of the Lord is very near. We know we live near the end, because God has placed so much evidence and proof in the world events around us—signs that are intended to alert us to the hour and the day in which we are living.

If the Jews of Jesus' day had only known the time of His coming, they would never have rejected Him. They would have received Him.

Actually, the Jews should have been looking for their Messiah to come the very year Jesus Christ entered Jerusalem. If they had been reading their Scriptures and had been properly taught the Word, they would have known exactly when the Messiah was due to appear.

Daniel had revealed that it would be 483 years from the time the commandment went forth to restore and rebuild Jerusalem to the coming of the Messiah the Prince. Since the commandment went forth in 445 B.C., the Jews should have been looking for their Messiah precisely when He arrived 483 years later. Daniel received this prophecy when he had been studying the Word of God. He knew that a dramatic year was arriving. Daniel knew through studying the Scriptures that the 70 years of the Jews' captivity in Babylon were about over, according to the prophecies of Jeremiah. Jeremiah 25:11 said, "[They] shall serve the king of Babylon seventy years." After some basic mathematics, Daniel knew the time of Israel's repatriation had come. He started praying and seeking the Lord concerning any special part He had for Daniel in the return of the people to the land.

Because Daniel was familiar with the Scriptures, he was aware of the world events around him. If you're in the Scriptures and studying the Word of God, then you should also be aware of the events that are happening in the world around you. You'll be privileged to know what they really mean!

The problem with the Jews in Christ's day was their lack of knowledge of the Scriptures. When Christ came they weren't expecting Him. They were expecting their King to come with regalia on a white charger or in a great chariot. But the Scriptures had said, "Behold, thy King cometh unto thee...lowly, and riding upon a [donkey]" (Zechariah 9:9). So, when Christ came riding on a donkey, they turned up their noses.

Today, we see people who are versed in so many areas of understanding, but they're totally oblivious to the fact that we're coming to the end of the line!

There is no reason why any believer should be taken by surprise when Jesus returns. Even as the Word of God gave so many signs and indications concerning His first coming, it also gives us many signs and indications of events that will be a forewarning of His second coming.

When I looked at the paper the other day, six of the seven articles on the front page were of prophetic significance! They were prophesied in the Scriptures as events at the time of the return of Jesus Christ. All around us are signs and indications that the coming of the Lord is at the door.

It's amazing to me that so many Christians are planning their lives as if they'll be here for at least another 20 years. Do I believe the Lord will return within 20 years? You bet your life I do! I don't want to be around 20 years from now, anyway. If what the ecologists say is true, it's going to be a very unpleasant world 20 years from now!

## Alerted

A young girl came up to me the other day and showed me her arm. There was a rash all over it. She said, "This is a fulfillment of Bible prophecy! I went to my doctor, and he said that this rash is a result of ultraviolet radiation. He said there are many cases of skin irritation due to ultraviolet radiation, because of the depletion of the ozone in the atmosphere."

If those who have been warning us about the dangers of aerosol propellants are correct and we continue to deplete the ozone blanket, 20 years from now you won't dare walk outside in the sun. If you decide to go to the store, you'll have to travel in a little mobile cubicle with protective shields (See Revelation 16:8–9).

But you're going to have a hard time propelling that little vehicle because, according to estimates, we'll be out of fossil fuels by then. And the experts haven't developed anything else which is even close to replacing fossil fuels as our major energy source.

According to an interesting book about these crises, scientists fed various factors and data regarding the world, its population, the food supply, the ability to grow food, etc., into a computer. Each time this information was fed into the computer to find out what the world would be like 20 years from now, the computer said, "The world can't last that long...there's not enough fuel to take you there...the ozone will be depleted to the point where life will be totally endangered...the population will be so large that you'll be unable to feed it."

Actually, 15 million people are dying of starvation this year. Two out of three people being born will suffer permanent brain damage from lack of protein in their diets during the developmental years.

There are the exotic super-weapons that are being developed. How much longer can we go until one of these is released by accident or on purpose? The terrorists in Europe are now talking about stealing a nuclear device and using it as their next threat of blackmail.

There are devices that might even be worse than the nuclear weapons. Our forces in Europe have been trained concerning a new nerve gas that has been developed by Russia. We have already received a kit with an anti-toxin for this gas. It contains a spring loaded needle. Hit yourself in any part of your body and the needle will go right through your boots or your clothing and inject this serum into your body. You have fifteen seconds from the time of exposure to the gas to inject the anti-toxin, or you'll be too late. You have ten seconds to analyze and determine whether or not you've been exposed to the gas. If you use the anti-toxin when you haven't actually been exposed to the gas, the anti-toxin will kill you.

What kind of a world are we living in when we have only ten seconds to judge, and if we make a mistake we lose our life? What kind of world will it be 20 years from now? And who wants to try to exist in that kind of world!

When you talk about the coming of the Lord, the world says, "You're a prophet of doom!" If you ask me, a gloomy message is what the ecologists are saying about our future. As I look around the world, I take great comfort in knowing that it won't be long until the Lord comes!

I look around and see the turmoil. I see, as the Scripture says, "distress of nations, with perplexity" (Luke 21:25). The word "perplexity" translated from the Greek actually means "no way out." We don't know what to do! The economic experts are as confused as the public. They don't want to admit it, because they're afraid we'll panic.

The Bible says that the night is far spent and the day is at hand (Romans 13:12a). The night of evil, the night of misery, the night of darkness of man's history is about over!

When I woke up just before dawn this morning, I looked outside. I could see vague outlines. I could make out the nearby trees. It was getting a little light in the eastern sky, just enough to see my way around. I knew that it wouldn't be very long before the sky would be getting brighter and brighter. And then the day would dawn. Now there was a sign and evidence. The faint light in the eastern sky told me that the day was at hand.

When my wife and I were awaiting our first child, we came to the day the doctor said would be the probable date of birth. But our child wasn't born. We waited another day. Still, she wasn't born. We waited a third day, and she wasn't born. I didn't throw down my hat and yell at my wife, "You deceived me! I don't think you're going to have a baby!" No. I still believed that our baby was coming. There were positive signs and evidences. I couldn't tell you the day or the hour. I didn't become an unbeliever just because it didn't happen the day we thought it was going to happen. In fact, with every day that went by we knew that the baby's arrival was more and more imminent.

The Lord must be coming any time now. We know that we're getting closer with each passing day. That's what

Paul meant when he said, "Now is our salvation nearer than when we believed" (Romans 13:11).

### Prepared

Realizing that the Lord's coming is due at any moment, how should we live in these final days of grace? First of all, Paul says that we should cast off the works of darkness. These works are described as rioting, drunkenness, chambering (sexual immorality) and wantonness (sexual immorality with no shame), strife and envying.

Christians living in this polluted world are under tremendous pressure. My mother used to say, "Son, any dead fish can float downstream with the current. It takes a live fish to swim upstream against the current." She said, "You'll be faced with a tide of evil, and the easy thing is to flow with it. But that only proves that you're spiritually dead." She said, "Be alive unto God. Be alive unto Jesus Christ. Dare to go against the tide!" Thank God for mothers who give that kind of advice to their sons.

Every once in a while, I hear my wife quietly sobbing. I go into the room to see what's wrong, and her hands will be over her face. She's a very beautiful and sensitive person. The newspaper will be in front of her. She's so sensitive to people and to suffering that, when she reads some of the things that are happening today, it just tears her up inside. My wife has too much empathy for the tragic victims of this crazy world in which we live. She cries for that little child who's been beaten or cruelly tortured and who doesn't even know why. Sometimes, I have to get up and turn off the television because her reaction is just too great. The stuff that people are doing is just so shocking that a sensitive person is completely torn up by it. It's sad to me that our children, being exposed to it for so long, have somehow built up an immunity to the violence of these days.

In light of these things, how should a Christian then live? "Let us put on the armor of light." The literal phrase in the Greek is "weapons of light."

Did you know that there are weapons of light? Truth is a powerful weapon of light. What a power the man has who uses the weapon of light in a dark and evil world, the man who will not bow his knee to Molech, the god of the flesh, but who stands strong in the face of the corrupt society around him.

Another powerful weapon of light is love. We're to put on love and let God's love fill our hearts and our lives.

What is destroying our whole system? Greed. We want someone else to make the sacrifices. Let someone else quit their driving. I'm not willing to sacrifice. Look at the whole economic upward spiral. Why? Because the laborers are demanding higher wages in order to buy the higher priced goods. The manufacturers are saying, "We've got to put higher prices on the merchandise so we can pay the higher wages." Greed drives inflation even higher.

Where's it going to end? It's almost over! The night is far spent. The glorious day of the Lord is at hand!

Paul next exhorts, "Put ye on the Lord Jesus Christ." He is the Light. Oh, that we will walk in His strength, His ability, and His power! It's only through Him that we have any chance at all in this world in which we're living. If you don't appropriate the power and strength of Jesus Christ, you're a goner!

If you believe you're only a product of accidental circumstances, a series of evolutionary changes, then life for you is meaningless. But life is real. Life is earnest. The grave is not the Christian's goal. Dust thou art, to dust returneth was not spoken of your soul!

God has a plan and a purpose for you. Put on the Lord Jesus Christ and discover the glorious life that God has for you. Life with meaning, a life of beauty, a life of joy, a life of love, as we walk in the Spirit, and as we, through Him, become a light in this black, darkened world.

Make no provision to fulfill your flesh's desires. Don't give it an opportunity. If you do, it can take over and bring you under its power and control. Knowing the time, it's high time that we wake up. It's almost over. The cry goes forth. "Behold, the bridegroom cometh" Jesus said to be ready!—for they that were ready went in to the marriage supper! (Matthew 25:6).

# CHAPTER 2

*Compared to the Heavens...*

# WHAT IS MAN?

One of the unfortunate by-products of our urbanized society with its resultant air-pollution and bright lights is that we cannot see the heavens very clearly anymore. I think that everyone who lives in an urban area should get away to the desert or mountains two or three times a year to look up and be reminded of the glory of heaven. Unfortunately, we forget about the vastness of the universe when we don't see it fully. We begin to think of this world as being closed-in, but when we look at the heavens, we can realize how great the creation of God is!

The Bible declares that the glory of God is greater than the heavens themselves. The psalmist David said,

> O Lord our Lord, how excellent is thy name in all the earth! who hast set thy glory above the heavens....When I consider thy heavens, the work of thy fingers, the moon and the stars, which thou hast ordained; What is man, that thou art mindful of him? (Psalm 8:1, 3–4).

The sun, the work of God's fingers, is 860,000 miles in diameter. It is so large that 1,200,000 Earths our size could be placed in it. Traveling at 11 1/2 miles per second through space, the sun was flung out by God's hand.

Many stars, because of the density of their atoms, weigh much more than the sun. One of the dual stars of Sirius has such a high density, the number of atoms in a given volume, that one cubic inch weighs 1,725 pounds! Imagine what would happen if a rock-sized meteor from Sirius was laying on the ground in your path and you decided to kick it out of the way. Yet, as heavy as that star is, God has also spun it into orbit.

Our sun is one of the billions of stars in the Milky Way Galaxy. This galaxy measures about 10,000 light-years wide and 100,000 light-years long. In other words, if you could travel on a beam of light at a speed of 186,000 miles per second, you could circle the Earth 7 1/2 times in just one second. Then, leaving the Earth at this speed, you could sail past the moon in 1 1/4 seconds and past the sun in 7 1/2 minutes. However, it would take you about 4 1/2 years to reach the nearest star, Alpha Centauri. To cross the width of the Milky Way Galaxy would take you 10,000 years and to cross the length would take you 100,000 years. If you then wanted to go to the nearest galaxy, Andromeda, you'd have to travel at the speed of light for 1 1/2 million years!

This vast universe contains billions of galaxies, one of which is the Milky Way Galaxy. In this galaxy there are billions of stars, and one of these stars we called the sun. Revolving around this star are the nine planets of the Solar System, one of which is called Earth. This planet is 7,926.7 miles in diameter at the equator, revolving around the sun at 19 miles per second, rotating on its axis at 1,000 miles per hour, traveling with the sun in its giant orbit at 11 1/2 miles per second, and (as some astronomers theorize) traveling at approximately 179 miles per second with the Milky Way. Imagine, as we just sit here all these motions are going on!

If you have ever spun a top, you know that it can spin for a long time, but ultimately it slows down and stops. I don't know how the Lord started the planet Earth spinning, but I do know He keeps it spinning—and it's not slowing down! God has ordained it and set it all in motion.

> When I consider thy heavens, the work of
> thy fingers, the moon and the stars, which thou
> hast ordained; What is man that thou art
> mindful of him?

This little planet Earth, as a part of a group of planets revolving around the sun, a part of a galaxy called the Milky Way, which is only one of billions of galaxies, contains billions of living creatures. Among these billions of living creatures is our species called man, of which there are almost four billion.

---

*God wants to bless you. Open your heart*
*and receive His love!*

---

It must have blown the mind of David when he realized that God's glory is greater than the heavens! He states,

> O Lord our Lord, how excellent is thy name
> in all the earth! Who has set thy glory above
> the heavens.

Then David added, "What is man, that thou art mindful of him?"

God is mindful of this little creature called man, on this little planet called Earth, in this little Solar System which is part of the Milky Way Galaxy, a part of this vast universe, all of which is the work of His fingers. The fact that God is mindful of me just amazes me! The Creator of this universe is conscious and mindful of me, His creation, here on this planet!

"What is man?" First of all, he is body. But the body elements aren't worth very much. With inflation, they are now probably worth about $2.26 in raw chemicals. Earlier, I made reference to the fact that the density of matter is determined by the atoms per unit volume. Our bodies are made up of atoms which have a nucleus of protons and neutrons with tiny electrons whirling around it. If you could stop these electrons from whirling, they would draw into the center of the mass of the nucleus. If all the atoms in your body collapsed like this, you would immediately disappear. There is so much empty space in these atoms that you'd be smaller than a speck of dust; in fact, it would take a microscope to see you. All of us are made up of these blown-up atoms.

However, the Bible teaches that man is more than body. It teaches that man is a soul and a *spirit*. The body is called a "tent" in the Scriptures, because it is the temporary dwelling place of the spirit. Paul the apostle said,

> For we know that if our earthly [tent] were
> dissolved, we have a building of God, an house
> not made with hands, eternal in the heavens (2
> Corinthians 5:1).

When these tents in which we're now living return to the dust from which they were made, by the grace of God, our spirits move out. God then has another place of habitation for our spirits—not tents, but houses.

> When I consider thy heavens, the work of thy fingers, the moon and the stars, which thou hast ordained; What is man, that thou art mindful of him?

God isn't mindful of me in some abstract way, He's mindful of me in a personal way. He knows when I get up in the morning and go to bed at night. He knows when some sound awakens me in the middle of the night. He knows my thoughts, and also understands my dusty frame (Psalm 103:14); and yet, knowing my weaknesses and my failings, He still loves me!

Sometimes, Satan lays a trip on us. He tells us that once we have made a mistake or failed, or because we may continually fail, God wants nothing to do with us. Satan would have us believe that God is no longer interested in us. But God knows our frames, that we are but dust. God also knows our hearts, and the real intentions of our hearts and lives.

When you have a little child who is just learning to walk, you let the child grasp on to your fingers to steady him as he walks. Then, when you feel that he's steady enough, you let go of his fingers. The child may really be attempting to take that first step, but he may fall right away, because he isn't coordinated enough to walk yet. When this happens, you don't pick him up and scold him, saying, "You rotten little kid! Why don't you walk?" You don't punish him for falling. You grab him and hold him close. You encourage him, saying, "That's okay, angel. Let's try again." You assure him of your love.

As long as the child is trying, you continue to encourage him and love him. Even though he may fail a hundred times, you don't toss the child out. You don't get rid of him just because he has failed. In the same way, God knows when you're trying; and, if you do fail, God doesn't discard you and say, "Oh, I get so sick of you!" He picks you up and holds you close, then dusts you off and says, "Come on now, let's try again."

On the other hand, you may have a teenager sitting in the room. If you say, "Come over here. I want to show you something," and he replies, "No, I don't want to, and you can't make me," you may want to pop his head off because he's being rebellious. There's a difference of attitude between the baby and the teenager. One is an attitude of weakness: wanting to do something but not being able to, the other is an attitude of rebellion: having the ability to do something and not wanting to. If you want to serve God but lack the ability, don't be afraid that God is going to be angry with you! God loves you! He knows your frame. He knows how uncoordinated you are spiritually. God looks upon us with love because we're His children. As a father pities his child who is learning to walk, so our heavenly Father looks upon us, His children, with pity.

However, if we're in open rebellion against God, saying, "I don't want to do it! I won't do it! You can't make me do it!" He may prove to us that He can make us do it, just as a father may prove to his teenage son that he can make him come across the room.

"What is man?" Generally, man is a rebellious little creature. He's down here on this little planet, shaking his fist at his Creator and saying, "I don't want to follow Your rules! I'll live just as I please! You can't make me live the way You want me to! I'll do what I want!" This is man, a little speck of dust, shaking his dusty fist at the Creator of the universe. How foolish it is to rebel against the Creator!

"What is man that thou art mindful of him?" The question is unanswerable. But God is not only mindful of me, He came to visit me: "And the son of man, that thou visitest him." The Gospel of John begins:

> In the beginning was the Word, and the Word was with God, and the Word was God. The same was in the beginning with God. All things were made by him; and without him was not any thing made that was made…. He was in the world, and the world was made by him and the world knew him not. He came unto his own, and his own received him not. But as many as received him, to them gave he power to become the sons of God, even to them that believe on his name…. And the Word was made flesh, and dwelt among us, (and we beheld his glory, the glory as of the only begotten of the Father), full of grace and truth (John 1:1–3, 10–12, 14).

God's visiting man is a marvelous mystery, but the blindness of man's rebellion is a tragedy. Rebellion will always blind you. It is always folly to be in rebellion against God. Here is little man rebelling against his Creator. His Creator came to visit him, but man didn't even recognize Him. Even though the world was made by Him, the world knew Him not.

Psalm 8 continues in prophecy of Jesus Christ and His visit to Earth.

> For thou hast made him a little lower than the angels, and hast crowned him with glory and honour. Thou madest him to have dominion

over the works of thy hands; thou hast put all
things under his feet.

In Hebrews 2:8 this Psalm is quoted in reference to Jesus
Christ. God has placed all things in subjection unto Jesus
Christ, giving Him the authority over all of His created
work. However, at the end of this passage the writer of
Hebrews declares, "But now we do not yet see all things
put under him."

---

*The heavens do declare the glory of*
*God... but only Jesus Christ declares the*
*fullness of God's love for man.*

---

As we look around in the world today, we do not see
everything in subjection to Jesus Christ. In fact, we see a
world in rebellion against His authority. Even as
Christians, our flesh sometimes rebels against Him, but
there is coming a day when God shall place all authority in
Jesus Christ. Every knee shall bow and every tongue shall
confess that Jesus Christ is Lord to the glory of the Father
(Isaiah 45:23; Romans 14:11; Philippians 2:10). We do not
yet see all things in subjection,

> But we see Jesus, who was made a little
> lower than the angels for the suffering of
> death, crowned with glory and honor (Hebrews
> 2:9).

May God help us to see beyond the rebellion around us
and beyond the rebellion of our own flesh, and may we,
this day, see Jesus! May we, this day, crown Him with
many crowns, the Lord upon His throne. May we, this

day, submit ourselves to His authority and to His will. May we bow our knee to His scepter and worship at His feet. May we enter into the glories of the kingdom of God by submitting ourselves to Jesus Christ, the King. May we see Jesus and, when we do, may we say with David, "O Jehovah our Lord, how excellent is thy name in all the earth! who has set thy glory above the heaven" (Psalm 8:1).

What is man that God would think of him? Yet He did. What is man that God should redeem him? Yet He has. What is man that God should want him? Yet He does. What is man that God should save him and make him His own throughout eternity? Yet He has!

The question we should be asking is not, "What is man?" but, "What is God?" He is infinite grace, infinite love, infinite goodness.

> For I know the thoughts that I think toward you, saith the LORD, thoughts of peace, and not of evil, to give you an expected end. Then shall ye call upon me, and ye shall go and pray unto me, and I will hearken unto you. And ye shall seek me, and find me, when ye shall search for me with all your heart (Jeremiah 29:11–13).

# CHAPTER 3

# POSITIVE CONFESSION

> And this is the confidence that we have in
> him, that, if we ask any thing according to his
> will, he heareth us: and if we know that he
> hear us, whatsoever we ask, we know that we
> have the petitions that we desired of him (1
> John 5:14–15).

The word *confidence* in the Greek literally means "the boldness of speech." When we talk to the Lord we can be bold! We can be free, open, and honest. If we say something wrong, it doesn't matter. God isn't going to throw it back at us. If we say something foolish, He understands. We can pray with real boldness of speech. Praying with confidence is an exciting thing!

The boldness of speech that we have is in asking. The Scripture has encouraged us to come boldly to the throne of grace that we might receive mercy in our time of need (Hebrews 4:16). That is proper and correct. There's nothing wrong with coming to God under pressure. I can't help but feel that maybe God at times has created the pressure just to get us to call on Him! There's nothing wrong with coming to God and asking. In fact, the Lord tells us to. Jesus said, "Ask, and it shall be given you"

(Matthew 7:7). Again, Jesus said, "Ask [please ask] and ye shall receive, that your joy may be full" (John 16:24).

When I come to God, I can come boldly. I can ask God for my needs. I don't have to worry that He'll misunderstand me. I don't have to be afraid that He'll be rude or rough with me. I don't have to worry that I might be asking the wrong thing.

We have this confidence in Him, "If we ask anything according to His will, He hears us." I'm so glad that qualification is there! I'm glad that this Scripture doesn't say, "Whatever we ask we receive." I'm very grateful that He inserted "according to His will." Had God answered all of my prayers, I wouldn't be here today. I would have destroyed myself a long time ago!

I have prayed for a lot of ridiculous things that would have totally ruined me. "According to His will" keeps a proper perspective between God and me. Any other way would remove the authority of God over my life. It would then mean that I was the master of my fate, the captain of my destiny. My life wouldn't be governed by God; instead, it would be governed by me.

If I can demand that God does anything, if I can lay out demands to which God must acquiesce because I'm demanding it in Jesus' name; or if I can just make positive confessions and start laying claims to things and, by my positive confessions, create situations and things for my life, then God is no longer in control of my life. I take control by the demands that I make upon God and by the confessions I make of these things. And God becomes the magic genie! I rub the lamp and God must come out to follow my orders.

Not so! God is far too loving for that. He loves you too much to let you run your life. When you put the "I" in "run," you've got the true picture: you'll "ruin" your life when you try to run it.

Paul tells us that we don't always know what the will of the Lord is. That's one of our problems in prayer. From past experience, I realize that I made so many mistakes in the analyses of my own needs that if God had answered some of those prayers, it would have been absolutely tragic!

What if I were in control? What if God were acquiescing to every confession that I made? People say, "Be careful not to make a negative confession! What you say is what you get." That's ridiculous!

David said, "I know one day Saul is going to kill me." Don't say that, David! That's negative confession. Now it's going to happen, because what you say is what you get! And now one day Saul is going to kill you. But Saul didn't kill David.

I have a good friend who's been saying for years, "I'll be a monkey's uncle." To my knowledge he hasn't become one yet.

"If I could have things by just making a positive confession." "If God must yield to my demands." Do you see what that immediately does? It elevates me to the position of God and puts God in the subservient position. I'm no longer serving God, but God is serving me and my every whim.

To put God in this kind of position, as Paul declares in Romans 1:21, is to fail to glorify God as God. It doesn't make God "God" anymore but some kind of servant who has to run around and do my will, follow my commands, and fill out my confessions. It puts me in control and God in the servant's seat. To exalt my demands, wishes, and my will above God's will is audacious, perverted, and insane.

Certainly, the greatest prayer any of us can ever pray is, "Not my will, but Thy will be done." That isn't a spiritual cop-out as some people would accuse. It's just glorifying God as God and recognizing that He's a lot smarter than I. I may *think* that something is best for me, but He *knows* what's best for me.

Behind every prayer I offer is an understanding with God that if I'm making a stupid request, He should *please* not honor it or answer it. I want God to do what's best for me or whatever is wisest in each situation. If you accuse me of a spiritual cop-out because I pray "Thy will be done," then you must also accuse Jesus Christ of a spiritual cop-out—because He's the source of the prayer!

"Not my will, but Thy will be done" is the wisest prayer I can offer to God. That's the way I always want it to be. Though I don't always articulate it, that submission to His will is always the background of every prayer I offer to God. "God, this is what I want. This is what I think I need. But, Lord, You know what I need better than I know myself. Your will be done in my life. Your will be done in this illness. Your will be done in this financial problem. Don't listen to me. I'll mess it up worse than it is. You do what is best for me, God."

A person who's afraid to pray "Thy will be done" is a person who doesn't truly understand or know God. If you really know God then you have no problems praying that way at all. Unfortunately, many people have a lot of false concepts of God.

Satan has done a tremendous job of lying about God and His nature. So many people think that God's will is the most terrible thing that could ever happen to them. They think that whatever you don't want to do is just what God will make you do when you say, "Thy will be done." If you say, "I don't want my nose rubbed in the dirt," the first thing that's going to happen is that God will rub your nose in the dirt. Oh, what a blasphemous concept of God to think that He would do some horrible, ugly thing just because you've submitted to His will. God's will for our lives is so glorious and marvelous that I'm afraid to have anything less than God's will for my life!

If God should come to me and say, "Chuck, I've been thinking about you lately. I'd like to do something special for you just to show you how much I love you"—what would I ask Him for? Oh, what will it be? Let's see...I might pay off the mortgage on my house. "Lord, what about twenty grand?" No. Before I get that far I'd stop. and say, "Lord, just give me whatever You want." You see, I might be thinking of twenty grand, but He might be thinking five hundred thousand! Why should I cut Him short?

God delights in giving good gifts to His children. He's more anxious to give than we are to receive! If you can have the proper concept of God then you can, with confidence, totally cast yourself upon Him and say, "Here I am, God! It's Your problem now! Take care of it. Whatever You want, whatever You wish. My life is Yours. You work out all the details and circumstances. I'm going to relax and let You do it!" You won't be able to believe those things He desires to do for your life—just because He loves you! No way am I afraid to say, "Lord, Thy will be done in this situation." That's all I want.

We must remember that there is a limitation to our asking: "...anything according to His will." The Scripture isn't just a blanket promise. God has put a limitation to our asking—a *blessed* limitation!

# CHAPTER 4

# THE HEALING DOCTRINE

### Can Healing Be Guaranteed?

Recently a woman, struggling awkwardly with her aluminum crutches, came up to me. An unfortunate victim of multiple sclerosis, she had tear-filled eyes that mirrored the pain in her heart. She asked, "How can I explain to my Christian friends that I still love the Lord and am not hiding sin in my life though I'm crippled like this?" My heart ached for her as I realized that she was one of the thousands of victims of the latest wind of doctrine sweeping across the church body today—the "Healing" doctrine.

Many evangelists and ministers have begun to proclaim a new doctrine that sounds more as though it came from the pen of Mary Baker Eddy than from the Bible. They're teaching that we must make only positive confessions of faith and should never confess to being sick or feeling ill, because our words are a powerful creative force and we become what we say. Thus, no matter what our sickness, if we make a confession of faith, we will become well. All illness, they assert, is a result of our negative confessions or lack of faith.

*Comforters, Old and New.* As with all false teachings, much of what this healing doctrine says is true. Many Christians today are guilty of harboring negative attitudes and defeatist complexes. I cannot deny that many people have been helped and healed by making a positive confession of faith. Yet, to say that it is God's will that none of His children be sick is wrong. And to say that they're sick because of a lack of faith, sin in their lives, or something amiss in their relationship with God is also wrong. I've known too many carnal Christians with marvelous health and too many deeply spiritual Christians with poor health to ever subscribe to such a heresy.

When I see the bad fruit from this doctrine, I can judge it to be *false*. I feel sorry for the couple who, at the encouragement of a healing evangelist, took their diabetic child off insulin and by faith began claiming his healing. When their child died they were charged with manslaughter, but the evangelist went free.

This doctrine has also led some beautiful saints of God to doubt their salvation because of their cancer. I've seen arthritics lose the joy of Christ because they were told something was lacking in their lives or faith which kept them in that painful condition. Tragically, those who are sick and in need of the greatest encouragement suffer the most from these extremist teachings.

Although in *some* cases a lack of faith may result in poor health, some of the Christians with the *greatest* faith and most positive attitudes have suffered physical maladies with no relief. Unquestionably, God does heal people today. Yet not *all* are healed.

I know of sinners who have received marvelous healings and of true saints who have died of cancer. I don't believe that death from a disease is necessarily a defeat; nor do I believe that if someone had offered the prayer of faith or had held on in faith then death would have been averted. Being a Christian or serving the Lord doesn't provide us with an immunity from sickness, the natural aging process, or death.

Since the time of Job, and perhaps before, men have sought to understand the problem of suffering and sickness and how it relates to our relationship with God. Job's friends, who came to comfort him, may have been gifted in worldly wisdom and philosophy, but they were ignorant of the ways of God. In the end, God rebuked Job's comforters for their counsel without knowledge and declared His anger against them, because what they said about God wasn't true. They had been telling Job that his problems came upon him because of a wrong relationship with God. If Job got right with God then all would be well in his life. But they failed to recognize, as do these modern false comforters, that God often allows suffering to work His purposes in our lives. I agree with Job: "Miserable comforters are ye all!"

It is heartless, unscriptural, and cruel to tell a person with a chronic sickness that he's not right with God, his confession of sickness is wrong, or he lacks faith. A couple whose son died of leukemia was told that if they'd only held on in faith their child would have been healed. They were told that their surrender to God by praying, "Thy will be done" made them responsible for their son's death. Another couple whose child had leukemia was encouraged to make positive confessions. They claimed the healing and refused to acknowledge the child's illness. When their child died they were spiritually destroyed. Some sicknesses persist because of a lack of faith, but not all. Some situations are helped by positive confessions, but not all.

*Scriptural Comfort.* In seeking to discover the truth about a doctrine we must turn to the Bible. When attempting to use the Scriptures to prove that God wants all of us to be healed, these false comforters point to 3 John 1:2; "I wish above all things that thou mayest prosper and be in health, even as thy soul prospereth." In context this verse is not an expression of God's will for all His saints. Rather, it is John's personal wish for his friend, Gaius.

In Mark 11:22–23 we read,

> And Jesus answering saith unto them, Have faith in God. For verily I say unto you, That whosoever shall say unto this mountain, Be thou removed, and be thou cast into the sea; and shall not doubt in his heart, but shall believe that those things which he saith shall come to pass; he shall have whatsoever he saith.

This is the basis for teaching the importance of someone making the right confession, with the emphasis on having whatever "he saith."

These questions then arise in my mind: Where does God's will come into the matter? Can I command God to work contrary to His own will? Is the purpose of prayer ever to get my will done? What kind of God would acquiesce to my demands doing for me what is contrary to His own will and what He knows to be bad for me, simply because I'm persistent in my demands?

Still, these modern-day "prophets" would have us feel guilty and accuse us of a lack of faith when we pray, "Thy will be done." But this prayer of commitment—resting my case with God's will—takes much *more* faith than demanding my own will to be done. If we're wrong in praying "Thy will be done," we're in good company. Jesus prayed it!

When we consider the relationship of our health to our faith, it is enlightening to look at Elisha, that Old Testament prophet of great faith. I don't know any other Old Testament saint who had more miracles of faith surrounding his life. Yet, we read in 2 Kings 13:14, "Now Elisha was fallen sick of his sickness whereof he died." Men of great faith also get sick. Paul wrote to Timothy not to drink water but to use a little wine for his stomach's problem and his constant weakness (1 Timothy 5:23). Paul also spoke of Epaphroditus, his brother and companion in the Lord's work, who was so sick he was "nigh unto death" (Philippians 2:27).

Although some of the Gospels speak of occasions where Jesus healed all that were sick, Mark's Gospel speaks of occasions where "many" were healed (Mark 1:32–34, 3:10). The inference is that not all were healed.

*Paul's Thorn in the Flesh.* In the history of the church one of the greatest leaders and men of faith was Paul the apostle. Yet, he testified of his own infirmity, his "thorn in the flesh" (2 Corinthians 12:7–10). During his ministry Paul had undergone a "life-after-death" experience. Paul himself says that he wasn't sure if he'd had a vision or if he'd really died. But Paul did know that he was caught up into heaven where he heard things so marvelous that it was unlawful for him to try to relate them in human language (2 Corinthians 12:1–4). As a result of the abundance of revelations, Paul also received a thorn in the flesh to keep him from being exalted above measure.

There is a constant danger for the man who is being used by God to begin to look to himself for the cause of God's blessings in his life. God is the source of every blessing that we receive—not because we're worthy or deserving, or because God can trust us. God bestows upon us such abundant mercy, grace and power only because He is gracious and merciful.

Paul warns everyone, "...not to think of himself more highly than he ought to think; but to think soberly..." (Romans 12:3). Whenever God begins to use us there's always that tendency to say, "I finally discovered the secret of faith!" (or the secret of commitment, or the secret of positive confession). We're always trying to point back to *ourselves* rather than to God's abundant, overflowing grace.

Pride is a very dangerous trap. In fact, it tops the list of things that God hates (Proverbs 6:16–17). It's also the sin that caused Satan's downfall. Proverbs warns, "Pride goeth before destruction..." (Proverbs 16:18a). Spiritual pride is the most damnable of all. "I'm holier than you. That's why God is able to use me. That's why God has touched me and has blessed me. I've done things right. You've done things wrong. That's why you're in the bad shape you're in." That concept is horrible and ugly!

If you receive any blessings from God—good health or a healing—don't look to yourself as the cause. The grace of God is the only cause of blessing. It's not because you believed or trusted. It's because God is gracious. Remember that.

Because of the abundance of revelations in Paul's life God put a thorn in his flesh to keep him from being puffed up. What was Paul's thorn in the flesh? The word "thorn" in the Greek actually means "a stake," a reference to a big tent stake. Don't think of Paul as having a little pesky thorn in his side. He had a tent stake driven in! It wasn't a minor irritation—it was a major disability!

Paul refers to his thorn as a "...messenger of Satan to buffet me." The word "messenger" in Greek is *aggelos*, which literally means "an angel." Paul had an angel of Satan to buffet him. His thorn in the flesh may have been a very painful eye disease causing his eyes to run continually. There are several allusions to this in the Scriptures (Galatians 4:15; 6:11). But whatever Paul's thorn was, it was an emissary of Satan who was continually buffeting him. Paul prayed for deliverance.

When Paul's thorn in the flesh originally came, he probably didn't think too much about it. "After all, I can always pray and trust God to heal me." But after he prayed and the problem still hung on, he began to think twice. "Lord. I asked You to heal me. Maybe You didn't understand, Lord. Get rid of this messenger from Satan! Stop him, Lord!" Paul prayed three times. But the weakness continued to persist. After the third prayer Paul received his answer. Was it deliverance from the thorn? No! He got something better. He received God's all-sufficient grace, power, and strength in his life!

God doesn't always give us what we ask. He oftentimes gives us more than what we ask. Many times the things we ask God to remove are the very instruments He uses to accomplish His purposes in our lives. God gave Paul an understanding of the thorn. "Paul, I'm going to allow you to be weak that you might constantly rely upon My strength. I'm going to allow this messenger of Satan to buffet you so that I might bestow upon you My all-sufficient grace" (2 Corinthians 12:8–9).

As we look at Paul we think, "What a shame. That's tragic. I don't know how you endured that, Paul." We offer our sympathies to Paul for this ugly thorn in the flesh. But

Paul answers, "Don't feel sorry for me. I take pleasure and glory in this weakness!"

Sometimes, you feel you've entered into real victory because you've learned to tolerate a condition in your body or in your own life. But God has something better for you. Don't just learn to live with it. Let it become the instrument of God's grace and power in your life. "Therefore I take pleasure in infirmities...for when I am weak, then am I strong" (2 Corinthians 12:10).

*Your Thorn.* Maybe today you're plagued by some thorn in your flesh. Maybe today you have comforters, as did Job, who are telling you to stop making negative confessions and to start making positive ones, "then things will be okay."

They say, "If you'll just believe and have enough faith, you'd be healed! Surely there's something wrong with you to be afflicted like this. Confess it to God and forsake your sin!" So you've confessed everything you can think of and you've made your positive confessions of faith—yet the thorn is still there.

Now Satan comes in and says, "God doesn't love you...If God loved you, surely you'd be well. If you were in the will of God this wouldn't be happening to you." So you begin to feel guilty, unloved, discouraged, and defeated because you don't know what's wrong. You don't know why the weakness persists.

Listen, God is saying, "Just trust in Me. My grace is sufficient for you, and My strength is made perfect in your weakness. I've got more for you than healing. *Receive today My abundant all-sufficient grace.*"

## A Gift Better Than Healing

God's ways are beyond our finding out. We'll never understand why some people are healed and others are not, why some notorious sinners enjoy marvelous health while some sincere Christians suffer from chronic illnesses.

To try to understand these things with our human reasoning places us in a dangerous position, as the Psalmist discovered in Psalm 73. He speaks about his feet almost slipping because he was tripped up by the health and prosperity of the wicked.

> But as for me, my feet were almost gone; my steps had well nigh slipped. For I was envious at the foolish, when I saw the prosperity of the wicked.

He began to draw the wrong conclusion: it doesn't pay to serve God.

It wasn't until he began to view these afflictions in the light of eternity that he was once again established. "Until I went into the sanctuary of God; then understood I their end." He received the assurance that God was indeed holding him, that God would guide him and afterward receive him into glory.

May we, with the psalmist, learn to commit our ways fully to God and stay close to Him. For, if He doesn't heal us, then He'll surely give us His all-sufficient grace to sustain us.

> Nevertheless I am continually with thee: thou hast holden me by my right hand. Thou shalt guide me with thy counsel, and afterward receive me to glory (Psalm 73:23–24).

# CHAPTER 5

# GOD'S REFINING PROCESS

Because the Jewish nation had forsaken the covenant of the Lord, walked in its own path, and would not harken to the Lord's voice, God proclaimed, through Jeremiah the prophet, the judgments to come against Judah. Jeremiah then turned to the Gentiles and prophesied the judgments to come against their nations.

Jeremiah 48 tells us that destructions are determined upon the Gentile nation of Moab. Its cities were to be made desolate. Its armies would be slaughtered and destroyed. Verse 11 tells us why:

> Moab hath been at ease from his youth, and he hath settled on his lees, and hath not been emptied from vessel to vessel, neither hath he gone into captivity: therefore his taste remained in him, and his scent is not changed.

## 1. Change

One thing that you must declare concerning the Gospel of Jesus Christ: it changes people. What you were before you met Christ is not what you are after you have met Him. "If any man be in Christ, he is a new creature: old things are passed away; behold, all things are become new" (2 Corinthians 5:17).

There is something radically wrong with the person who claims to know Jesus Christ and has not had any changes in his life—who still walks after and according to the things of the flesh and minds the things of the flesh— because Jesus Christ will change your life. You cannot be the same person after you have met Him if you have truly experienced His power in your life.

One of the sad testimonies of the church is that many of the people who attend church, take the name of Christian, and say their prayers faithfully have never had the change in their lives that Christ effects in a man.

The basic difference between a Christian and a non-Christian is that the non-Christian is ruled by his flesh and by his fleshly desires. In talking about our pre-Christ experience, Paul the apostle said:

> In time past ye walked according to the course of this world, according to the prince of the power of the air, the spirit that now worketh in the children of disobedience; among whom also we all had our conversation in times past in the lusts of our flesh, fulfilling the desires of the flesh (Ephesians 2:2–3).

A person who hasn't met Jesus Christ is a person whose life is dominated by his flesh and fleshly desires. A person who has come to the lordship of Jesus Christ is a person who knows and acknowledges the supremacy of the Holy Spirit and lives according to the Spirit. The Bible tells us, "As many as are led by the Spirit of God, they are the sons of God" (Romans 8:14).

It's possible to call Jesus "Lord." It's possible to have all the religious vernacular, go to church, sit and listen to the messages, but never be touched in the deeper area of your life. You may have the head knowledge. You may have the spiritual jargon down pat. But if it hasn't come into the area of your life where it affects your will, your religion is vain.

---

*God's refining process is based on love!*
*He won't let us stay settled in the dregs of*
*the flesh. He has something better*
*for us than the empty, fruitless*
*life we often seek.*

---

If you're not being led by the Spirit of God, you're not a son of God. You're still mastered and dominated by your flesh and still living after the flesh. The Bible declares that the mind of the flesh is sin and death, but the mind of the Spirit is life, peace, and joy in the Holy Ghost (Romans 8:6).

You can't go out all week sowing wild oats, then come to church on Sunday and pray that they'll never grow. "Oh, God, kill all the seeds I've sown this week! Don't let them grow." That can't happen. "Be not deceived; God is not mocked, for whatsoever a man soweth, that shall he also reap" (Galatians 6:7). If you're living to the flesh and sowing to the flesh, of the flesh you're going to reap corruption.

Jesus was crucified for making this declaration. He asserted the supremacy of the spiritual over the material.

The people couldn't handle it, and they finally put Him to death. Yet it's true. When Jesus Christ comes into your life He changes you from the flesh-ruled life to the Spirit-ruled life.

Jesus said, "If any man will come after Me, let him deny himself..." (Matthew 16:24). That's the very first step. You've got to deny the old life, the old flesh, the desires of the flesh. Deny "himself" is the very first thing. Many people have come to Jesus Christ in theory, but they haven't yet come to Him in practice. They're saying, "Lord, Lord," but they're not obedient to the will of the Father.

### 2. Purification

The second thing the Gospel of Jesus Christ does to a person is purification. The Bible says that we are pure even as He is pure (1 John 3:3). God is going to work in your life to purify you. God wants to bring you into purity. This purifying work is explained in Jeremiah 48:11, where he is describing the process by which wine is made. Jeremiah said that Moab had been at ease from his youth, had settled on his lees, and had never been poured from vessel to vessel. This was his problem. Moab had never been disturbed.

When they were making wine, the people would pour the juice into a vessel. They would allow it to set in that vessel until it fermented. The sediment, known as lees or dregs, would settle to the bottom of the vessel. Once the dregs settled, they would carefully pour the wine out of that vessel into another vessel, so that the settling process might again take place. As the dregs sank to the bottom, the wine makers would pour the liquid back into another vessel. Back and forth from vessel to vessel, each time being careful not to pour out the dregs. They were coming to a pure, clear product of the vine. This was their method of making excellent wine.

If the people didn't pour the wine from vessel to vessel but allowed it to set too long in the collected dregs, the fermented juice would begin to develop the taste of the dregs. The wine would become bitter. Then it would begin to get the smell of the dregs, a rotten smell. It would also begin to take on the color of the dregs. It's tragic when Christians get settled in the things of the flesh, the flesh walk, the flesh life. At one time in their Christian walk they were shocked that people could do such evil things of the flesh. They'd say, "I would never do that!" After a while, you find them doing the same things and becoming settled in them.

This impurity actually begins to permeate your whole life. Your life begins to be *colored* by the flesh. Your life begins to *smell* of the things of the flesh. Your life begins to just *taste* of the things of the flesh. Rather than bringing spiritual refreshment, all you're talking about is the latest chatter of what's happening here, what's happening there, this new movie, that new fashion. Your mind is caught up in the things of the flesh. In reality, you become no more than a heathen. Jesus said that you shouldn't be taking thought about what to eat, what to drink, or what to wear. He said, "For after all these things do the Gentiles [the heathen] seek" (Matthew 6:31–32).

If your life gets caught up in that trip—what shall we eat, what shall we wear, what new thing to buy, always interested in the adornment of your body, buying clothes and keeping up with the fashions, or always in the eating and drinking crowd, seeking to delight yourself in the fancy foods, a gourmet—you're no better off than the heathen. These things occupy their minds. They live after the flesh.

It's tragic when Christians settle down in these kinds of dregs so much that their lives are colored by it. You can't have a spiritual conversation with them. They're so interested in some new thing they purchased last week— "Wait till you see it!" It's all a flesh trip. Settling in the dregs of the flesh, they are colored, they are scented, they are tasting of the things of the flesh. It is a flesh life, not the life of the Spirit. God wants to purify us. God wants to clean out those dregs. God has something better for you than that empty, fruitless life of the flesh. You need to experience the purifying effect of the Gospel of Jesus Christ!

It's tragic that many people who have spent their entire lives in church or under its influence, attending very regularly, are still spiritually "babes in Christ." Paul calls them "carnal" (1 Corinthians 3:1–4). They've never developed in their spiritual walk. They've been at ease. They've settled into the dregs. They haven't been poured from vessel to vessel.

### 3. Deliverance

The third thing the Gospel of Jesus Christ accomplishes is deliverance. The power of Jesus Christ can set you free from the power of the flesh. Some of you today have become slaves to your fleshly desires. It's amazing what a strong grip and hold it can get on your life. The very first time you tried it, it was just for a kick. You were just searching for a little diversion.

We have many people in our church who are alcoholics. How little did they realize the power it would get on their lives, the grip it would hold over them. Thank God they know now. They know better than to take again that first drink. They've experienced the delivering power of Jesus

Christ. Having been delivered from the entanglements of the world, don't be so foolish as to go back and be entangled again with that yoke of bondage.

---

*Unless we're poured from vessel to vessel, our lives begin to "smell" of the things which we have settled into!*

---

We have many drug addicts. Maybe the first time they took a pill was to ease the appetite a bit. Maybe it was to alleviate some pain or to calm their nerves. But the drug began to get a hold of them until, finally, they came under the power of that substance, unable to free themselves. They found themselves bound in that drug. How little did so many realize, when they took that first fix, the hell it was leading them into.

They know now. Thank God for the power of Jesus Christ to deliver us from the bondage of corruption in which we found ourselves through our own folly and foolishness. The power of Jesus Christ can and does deliver man from the bondage of sin and death.

Today, maybe you find yourself entangled in a situation where you never thought you'd be. Maybe today you find yourself caught up in an adulterous situation. It started off so innocently, just as a little flirtation. Now, you're all involved. You never intended to be, but you opened the door to the flesh, and it took over. Now that situation is mastering your life. The Gospel of Jesus Christ can set you free. He can deliver you. Maybe you're hooked on drugs, or maybe you can't stop drinking. You've come to the place where you need that shot when you get home in the evening. Then, worse, you need it when you get up in the morning.

Maybe you have been bound by some desire or lust that has overwhelmed you and made you its victim. Moab was in this sad condition, because it had been at ease. Moab never had any problem, never was in captivity, never knew what it was all about. It grew up rather sheltered and protected. It settled into this condition as a result of no waves, no stirring. Moab had never been poured from vessel to vessel.

But, you know, God loves you. If you come to that place in your Christian experience where you start to relax and settle down into the dregs of the flesh, God's love won't allow you to get by with it. God will upset your position. Maybe someone who is very dear to us, someone we've come to rely upon, is suddenly taken away. "Oh, God, why is he gone? What are you doing, Lord?" He's now pouring you from vessel to vessel.

Maybe the boss suddenly says, "Hey, we're going to transfer you to Spokane."

"Spokane?" you say. "I don't know anybody in Spokane! All my friends are here. My children are in school here." A total uprooting—new friends, new associates, new environment, new schools. You cry out, "What are you doing God?" He's causing you to trust and rely upon Him. God is going to strip you of whatever has created your ease. Maybe it's your retirement, maybe it's your possessions, maybe it's your bank account. You've settled at ease in these things, your lees. But God doesn't want you to be dominated by your flesh. God will deliver you from the bondage of corruption.

God uses disturbances. They are the tools of God to bring us to Himself, to take away our trust and our reliance in other things. He doesn't want us to have job security, social security or security in man, government, bank accounts, or ourselves. He wants us to find our total security in Him. And so He pours us from vessel to vessel.

---

*For the mind of the flesh is death, but*
*the mind of the Spirit is life and peace*
*(Romans 8:6).*

---

Maybe this knowledge has disturbed some of you. Praise the Lord! You see, He wants to shake you up from that little smugness and ease in the flesh that you've fallen into, the trap of trying to find the answer in the things of the flesh.

We have been created for His pleasure (Revelation 4:11). He can't enjoy us when we smell of the flesh. He can't enjoy us when we taste of the flesh. *It is only as we walk in the Spirit, as we live in the Spirit, as we move in the Spirit, that we become what God would have us be—a pure product that He can enjoy.*

## A Time of Change

You go to work. The foreman walks up to you and says, "I don't know what's wrong, but here's your termination notice." You think, "Termination? What do you mean *termination?* I've got house payments, car payments, and television payments. What do you mean *termination?* Oh, God! What are You doing?"

He's got your attention now. He's pouring you from vessel to vessel. You see, you began to rely on and find security in your job. You were settling down into the dregs. You weren't walking after the Lord. You weren't searching after the *Spirit.*

God doesn't want you to smell of the flesh. So, God pours you into another vessel. God will not let you get entangled in the things of the flesh. If you start doing it, if you start meddling, if you start giving over to the things of the flesh, your day is coming. God is going to pour you from vessel to vessel to purify you.

And, suddenly, there you are. You're brought into a new relationship with God—being refined and purified through these disturbances that He brings into our lives.

# CHAPTER 6

# KEEP YOURSELF IN THE LOVE OF GOD

Jude exhorts us: "Keep yourselves in the love of God" (v. 21). This seems like a strange injunction. If you don't read the entire context, you could easily misinterpret it. How can we keep ourselves in the love of God?

Looking back at verse one, however, we find that Jude is writing to those who are "preserved" or kept in Jesus Christ and have been "sanctified" and "called" by God. Jude shows throughout this short letter that some have begun in fellowship with God, but have failed to keep themselves in the love of God. Thus, they haven't achieved the full potential of God's plan for their lives. They failed to keep themselves in that place where God could bless them.

Jude writes about the children of Israel who, though delivered out of Egypt, perished in the wilderness (v. 5). They didn't enter into the full blessing God had for them, because they didn't keep themselves in the love of God. Though they had experienced deliverance, they didn't come to the full benefits of God's work in their lives. They failed to keep themselves in the love of God.

Jude also describes certain angels who once were in fellowship with God and abode in His kingdom, but they "kept not their first estate" (v. 6). They didn't keep themselves in the love of God and were cast out of His kingdom. Now they are reserved for the day of judgment.

The people of Sodom and Gomorrah, who lived in that well-watered area of the plain, had many blessings from the hand of God; yet, they certainly didn't appreciate them (v. 7). They didn't keep themselves in the love of God and, thus, failed in their purpose for life.

Jude mentions Cain, who killed his brother; Balaam, who enticed the people of God to sin; and Korah ("Core" in the Greek translation), who rebelled against the authority of God and was destroyed (v. 11). With this background the writer exhorts us, "Keep yourselves in the love of God."

What did he mean by that? First of all, we know what he didn't mean. He didn't mean to keep yourself in such a way as to make God love you. He didn't mean for you to do nice things for God's love. God's love is unsought, undeserved, and unconditional. You cannot get away from the love of God. God loves you just as you are. You may be in the midst of rebellion against God today, but He still loves you. God isn't persuaded to love you because you're an especially good person. The text doesn't mean that—because you cannot put yourself outside of the love of God!

John 3:16 begins, "For God so loved the world." The world that God loved wasn't seeking His love, nor did it deserve His love. Yet God did love it. God didn't impose conditions on the world. He didn't say, "Now, if you fulfill these conditions, I'll love you." God loved the world as it was, in the midst of rebellion against His order and His government. He loves it still.

---

*We can lose that first glow of having our hearts aglow with God's love and of desiring nothing else but Him by not keeping ourselves in His love.*

---

God, because He loves you, wants to demonstrate that love by bestowing His blessings upon your life. Jude points out three attitudes in verse 11 that can *restrict* God's blessings. Cain hated his brother. Balaam was mastered by greed, thus he enticed the people of God to sin. Korah was envious, which led to rebellion against the government of God. You may be thinking, "Oh, you're talking about murder, enticing people to sin, and rebellion against God's established order. You're not talking about *me*." But Jesus in His Great Manifesto said,

> Ye have heard that it was said by them of old time, Thou shalt not kill;...but I say unto you, That whosoever is angry with his brother without a cause shall be in danger of the judgment (Matthew 5:21–22).

John stated, "Whosoever hateth his brother is a murderer" (1 John 3:15).

Cain killed his brother after coming home from offering a sacrifice to God (Genesis 4:3–8). Cain had just been to church! Yet, his heart was filled with hatred toward Abel and he murdered him. *Hatred* is not in harmony with love. Keep yourself from hatred.

Balaam enticed the people of God to sin, because he was filled with greed (Numbers 22–24). He desired the rich reward that Balak the king had offered. Though Balaam couldn't curse the people of God, he enticed them into a trap that brought a curse upon them. He did this right after uttering one of the most beautiful prophecies in the Old Testament! It was an anointed, inspired prophecy concerning the people of God. Then Balaam betrayed the people by telling the king how to entice them into sin, so that God's judgment would fall upon them. *Greed* is out of harmony with the love of God. Keep yourself from greed.

Korah was filled with envy because of Aaron and the appointed priesthood (Numbers 16). Korah was a leader among the people and a leader of a popular movement. He was a minister of God and offered services unto God, and yet he was envious of the high position of others. So whatever he had was taken away from him. *Envy* is out of harmony with love. Keep yourself from envy.

Keep yourself from hatred, greed, and envy, for these things are out of harmony with love. If these things fill your life, you cannot enjoy the fullness of the benefits that God wants to bestow upon you. Those rich blessings cannot be given to you if these evil things are hindering what God wants to do. Keep yourself in the love of God. This warning is needed, because sometimes we're in danger of losing that first bloom of love. We can lose that first glow of love when Jesus came in to our lives and washed away all our sins. We can lose that feeling of having our hearts aglow with His love and of desiring nothing else but Him— by not keeping ourselves in His love.

Jesus wrote to the church at Ephesus:

> I know thy works, and thy labor, and thy
> patience, and how thou canst not bear them

> which are evil: and thou hast tried them
> which say they are apostles, and are not,...and
> hast not fainted. Nevertheless I have
> somewhat against thee, because thou hast left
> thy first love (Revelation 2:2–4).

The first bloom of love had gone! The glow of fresh love wasn't there anymore. Jesus warned them of the inevitable consequences of leaving that first love. He said it would ultimately result in the candlestick's removal from its place—the loss of the consciousness of the presence of Jesus Christ.

If that love of the Lord isn't burning brightly in your heart, one day you'll even lose the consciousness of God's presence. The Bible says, "In thy presence is fulness of joy" (Psalm 16:11). But with the loss of the consciousness of His presence comes the loss of the joy in your life. You wonder, "What's happening to me? Where is the *blessing* I once knew? Where is the *joy* I once had?"

Your problem is that you haven't kept yourself in the love of God. You have allowed *hatred, greed,* or *envy* to come in. It has robbed you of what God wants to do and what He already has done. Only by keeping yourself in God's love can you blossom into the full potential God has for you—and for which He's drawn you out from the world and the bondage of sin.

Grace doesn't act independently of responses. Though God's grace is extended toward you, you must *respond* to the grace of God if you're to benefit from that grace. Privilege brings responsibility—and responsibility not acted upon can destroy you.

God's Word is searching your heart right now, and if you're in His love, respond to it. Put away all that is *contrary* to the love of God—any bitterness, any hatred, any impurity—and keep yourself *in* the love of God!

*Q. How can I keep myself in the love of God?*

**A.** Right here surrounding our text Jude gives us three steps for keeping ourselves in the love of God.

**1.** "But ye, beloved, building up yourselves on your most holy faith" (v. 20). As we read this epistle, we realize Jude is talking about faith in Jesus Christ as the Messiah, the Savior of the world. In the beginning of the letter he warns about those who will even deny our Lord Jesus Christ (v. 4). So, building up your faith in Jesus Christ is the first and foremost means of keeping yourself in the love of God. Jesus Christ is the *foundation* upon which we build.

Peter said,

> Thou art the Christ, the Son of the living God. And Jesus answered and said unto him, Blessed art thou, Simon Barjona: for flesh and blood hath not revealed it unto thee, but my Father which is in heaven. And I say also unto thee, that thou art Peter, and upon this rock I will build my church (Matthew 16:16–18).

What is the "rock" that Christ builds His church upon? The fact that *Jesus* is the Christ, the Son of the living God, the Savior of the world. This is the foundation upon which to build your faith.

Paul the apostle said, "For other foundation can no man lay than that is laid, which is Jesus Christ" (1 Corinthians 3:11). Build your faith upon this *foundational rock of Jesus.* For Jesus Christ was with God, He is God, but He became flesh and dwelt among us (John 1:1–2, 14). He went to the cross, carrying upon Himself all our sin and guilt, and He died in our place—but He rose again the third day. He ascended to heaven to the Father where He lives today, making intercession for you and me. This is the foundation. Now build on it in faith!

**2.** Jude 20 continues, "praying in the Holy Ghost." What does that mean? "Praying in the Holy Ghost" means that your prayers are directed by the Holy Spirit. So many of our prayers are directed by our own needs, by our own intellects, or by our own wishes and desires. Jude is encouraging us to pray in the Holy Ghost.

---

*If that love of the Lord isn't burning brightly in your heart, one day you'll even lose the consciousness of God's presence.*

---

In Romans 8, Paul talks about one of the weaknesses that we have as Christians:

> Likewise the Spirit also helpeth our infirmities: for we know not what we should pray for as we ought: but the Spirit itself maketh intercession for us with groanings which cannot be uttered (Romans 8:26).

One of our weaknesses is that we don't always know how to pray. But the Spirit, he said, will make intercession, because He knows what the mind of the Father is, and intercedes according to His will.

How can you pray in the Holy Ghost? You can pray in the Holy Ghost when, out of your deepest being, you can no longer adequately express yourself to God. Savonarola, a 15th Century reformer, said, "When prayer reaches its ultimate, words are impossible." You move from the realm of the intellect into the realm of the Spirit, and you let God interpret your prayer. It may come forth in soft weeping or as a groan. Your praying may be totally unintelligible to you, but it is communion with God in the deepest sense. Through it God washes, purifies, and cleanses your soul and keeps you in His love.

Paul declares,

> For if I pray in an unknown tongue, my spirit prayeth, but my understanding is unfruitful. What is it then? I will pray with the spirit, and I will pray with the understanding also (1 Corinthians 14:14–15).

The obvious reference with praying in the Spirit is when we're praying in an unknown tongue. Such praying in the Holy Spirit keeps us in the love of God.

**3.** The third way to keep ourselves in the love of God is to look "for the mercy of our Lord Jesus Christ unto eternal life" (v. 21). We keep ourselves in the love of God by looking for the return at any moment of Jesus Christ. The consciousness that Jesus might come *today* makes me very concerned with what I say, how I preach, and how I relate His truth.

If you're witnessing with the realization that this might be the last opportunity to share Jesus Christ with this person, you'll be very careful about how you witness to him. If you realize this might be your last day to serve the Lord, you'll be careful about how you serve Him. You'll want to do it in such a way that you'll be in full harmony with His love and His Spirit. There's nothing like the expectancy of the return of Jesus Christ to channel the church into holy, righteous living.

Jesus warns in His Word,

> For when they shall say, Peace and safety; then sudden destruction cometh upon them (1 Thessalonians 5:3).

Jesus is coming at any moment! "Unto them that look for him shall he appear the second time" (Hebrews 9:28). Be looking for the return of your Lord. Don't get caught up in the "Lord delayeth His coming" syndrome. Don't get caught up in the things of the world.

Live in harmony with God's love, so that you can become the full recipient of all the blessings, grace, and goodness that come from walking in fellowship with God and in His love. Having begun in the love of God, don't depart from the love, and thus, miss the full benefits of it. Don't wander in the wilderness when you can be resting in an oasis, enjoying the fullness of God in your life. "Keep yourselves in the love of God."

Jude began his epistle by addressing those who are kept or preserved in Jesus Christ. He ends his epistle by praising, "him that is able to keep you from falling, and to present you faultless" (v. 24). The chief injunction of the epistle is: keep yourselves in the love of God.

---

*You cannot get away from the love of God.*
*God loves you just as you are.*

---

One day Christ will present you faultless before the presence of God's glory. But you must *respond* to that grace of God. You must keep yourself in that place where God can bless you and use you. Keep your heart from hatred, greed, and envy—those evils that would choke out God's work in your life. Keep yourself in the love of God—and He will keep you unto that day!

### Does God still love me?

A little boy asked his Sunday school teacher, "Does God love bad little boys?"

The teacher answered, "Oh, no. God doesn't love bad little boys—just good little boys."

But this reply is wrong. In fact, it's blasphemous. God loves bad little boys. God loves bad little girls, too. He loves everyone! Somehow, we think, "Well, because I've been bad, God doesn't love me anymore." That's not true! God loves you just as much when you're bad as when you're good—for God's love is unconditional. Though you may have wandered from God, grieved God, or even forgotten God, His love is still reaching out toward you.

So, why does the Scripture say, "Keep yourselves in the love of God"? You must keep yourself in a position of harmony with God's love, so that you can receive and enjoy its full benefits and blessings. Though God loves the world today, much of the world receives no direct benefits of His love. Indirectly, everyone benefits from God's love. For example, everyone enjoys the sunshine—those who love God and those who don't. We love God, but not everyone does. We're in harmony and fellowship with God's love, but others are not.

Today, you may be living beneath the full, rich benefits that God has for your life. The Israelites wandered in the wilderness for forty years, as a result of their rebellion against God and the rejection of His love. But Isaiah 9 tells us, "His hand is stretched out still" (v. 12). They spited the love of God, but "His hand is stretched out still" (v. 17).

Just as the children of Israel, you may have been delivered out of Egypt, but may still be wandering in the wilderness. You haven't entered into the full benefits of God's promises. Though this glorious inheritance is waiting for you, you may still be a spiritual pauper.

The full benefits of God's love cannot be manifested in your life if you're not keeping yourself in the love of God. You dwell in the love of God, but only when you live in harmony with the love of God will you begin to experience the abundant richness and fullness of that love.

# CHAPTER 7

# TWO FALSE DOCTRINES

### Shepherding or Dictatorship?
### and
### Christian "Possession"

### Sound Doctrine

Paul the apostle exhorted both Timothy and Titus about sound doctrine. To Timothy he said:

> For the time will come when they will not endure sound doctrine; but after their own lusts shall they heap to themselves teachers, having itching ears; and they shall turn away their ears from the truth, and shall be turned unto fables (2 Timothy 4:3, 4; see 1 Timothy 1:10; Titus 1:9; 2:1).

What is the only true criterion for sound doctrine? **God's written Word.** The words of spiritual teachers or "spiritual" experiences must never supersede the Word of God. Paul said,

> But though we, or an angel from heaven, preach any other gospel unto you than that

59

which we have preached unto you, let him be accursed (Galatians 1:8).

The relating of experiences which are *fables* can never be the true basis for sound doctrine. The minute that we open the door and begin to teach from experience, we lose authority and introduce confusion. People have a great variety of experiences. If I accept one unscriptural experience as evidence for doctrinal truth, then I am bound to accept all experiences—for each one would have equal authority as a basis for doctrine.

## *"Shepherding"*

The doctrine of submission, covering, apostleship, or shepherding (or any of the numerous terms by which it is known) basically teaches that you must submit yourself to an elder or a group of elders within the Body of Christ, oftentimes called "shepherds." You cannot make any major decision without their prior approval.

If you want to buy or sell your house, it's imperative that you first consult your elder. He will tell you whether or not you can buy or sell. The same is true if you want to buy or sell a car or TV, or if you want to change your job. If you want to go on a trip, these shepherds will tell you where you can go, how long you can stay, and when to be back. They seek to exercise *complete authority and control* over your life.

If you desire to move to another locality, they'll tell you whether or not you may have their blessings and permission. You must submit to the shepherds in all the areas of your life that they deem important and necessary. To refuse to do so is to be marked as a rebel.

The elders have set up an apostleship. The apostle has absolute and complete authority over those under his apostleship. Though he may have "elders" under his apostleship, he has the power to overrule any decision that they make individually or collectively.

On many occasions these shepherds have told a person exactly whom he or she was to marry, how much and when to give, what books to read, and which tapes to listen to. Your elder or shepherd becomes spiritually responsible for your life.

They teach that it is absolutely imperative to obey your elder—even if he is wrong. If you'll submit to and obey him, you'll be all right. What you do will be right, because you've done it in obedience to your elder. *He* is your covering: responsible to God for you and your actions.

In some areas this doctrine teaches that when you have led someone to Jesus Christ, you automatically become this person's shepherd. Therefore, you're not to witness or lead anybody to Christ until you're spiritually mature enough to shepherd them. Your shepherd will inform you when you have achieved that spiritual maturity. In the meantime, they emphasize that you should wait and get your act together—become perfected yourself. Once you're perfected, then you'll be able to witness.

As a result of this teaching, these elders have sterilized some who were formerly dynamic in their witness for Jesus Christ. Men who had a powerful ministry and were being used of God have been placed on the shelf. Their shepherds told them that they weren't mature enough to minister yet. They ought to stop and get their own marriages together, or get their own lives together, before seeking to serve the Lord in any capacity. I personally know of many who have been neutralized in their effectiveness for Christ as the result of this doctrine.

This shepherding doctrine also teaches that all your tithes belong to your shepherd. He, in turn, pays his tithes to his shepherd, who pays his tithes to his shepherd. It's a neat chain-letter if you're sitting on top of the pile! Someone asked, "Where did this doctrine originate?" I'm sure it originated in hell, but it came out of Florida from the same group that teaches that Christians can be demon-possessed and need exorcism. In some services they passed out Kleenexes so people could regurgitate their demons of gluttony, lust, pride, anger, temper—all works of the flesh that they were calling demons.

### Elder's Position

Let's see what God's Word has to say concerning "shepherding" or lordship within the church. First of all, in his epistle to Philemon, Paul wrote:

> Wherefore, though I might be much bold in Christ to [order] thee that which is convenient, yet for love's sake I rather beseech thee (vv. 8, 9).

Philemon was Paul's own convert. He owed much to Paul. Yet, Paul didn't seek to exercise his authority over him (concerning the runaway slave, Onesimus). Instead, Paul beseeches Philemon through the love of Jesus Christ.

In speaking to the Corinthian church, Paul said,

> Not for that we have dominion over your faith, but are helpers of your joy: for by faith ye stand (2 Corinthians 1:24).

Paul is declaring that he doesn't have and doesn't seek dominion over the faith of the believers.

---

*There is one mediator between God and men—Jesus Christ. For any other person to take that position or role is scripturally wrong.*

---

The apostle Peter wrote to the elders, the "shepherds" who are in some of the churches today seeking to exercise this lordship and authority: "The elders which are among you **I exhort**, who am also an elder, and a witness of the sufferings of Christ, and also a partaker of the glory that shall be revealed." Peter said, "I exhort"—not "I order."

> Feed the flock of God which is among you, taking the oversight thereof, not by constraint (that is, not by forcing them), but willingly; not for filthy lucre, but of a ready mind; neither as being **lords** over God's heritage (the flock of God), but being [examples] to the flock. And when the chief Shepherd shall appear, ye shall receive a crown of glory that fadeth not away. Likewise, ye younger, submit yourselves unto the elder (1 Peter 5:1–5).

You say, "There's scriptural support for the doctrine right there!" But notice what Peter says in the rest of the verse: "Yea, all of you be subject *one to another*, and be clothed with humility."

Peter is declaring that the elders aren't to lord over God's heritage. That particular Greek word for "lord" is used elsewhere in the New Testament. It means "to rule over, to bring into subjection or submission." Don't try to bring the flock into submission or subjection to the shepherd.

### Priesthood

In Revelation 2, we find Jesus speaking to the church of Ephesus. He had some heavy things to say about the problems in the church; basically, that they had left their first love. But in verse 6 Jesus had a word of commendation:

"But this thou hast, that thou hatest the deeds of the Nicolaitanes, which I also hate." The word "Nicolaitanes" in the Greek actually speaks of the establishment of a spiritual hierarchy. *Nikao*: to establish a priesthood over, to conquer. *Laos*: the laity. The "deeds of the Nicolaitanes" was the establishment of the priesthood over the laity.

Establishing shepherds or elders who lord over the flock of God and make you responsible to them—who seek to take the spiritual responsibility for your actions by telling you what you can and can't do, when you can or can't do it, and have you come to them for guidance and direction—is, in reality, the doctrine of Nicolaitanes. In essence, these shepherds are saying, "You can't go to God for directions. You're not mature enough. You come to me, and I'll tell you what God says." And that is inserting someone between man and God.

Jesus Christ paid a tremendous price to open the door to God for every man. "Let us therefore come boldly unto the throne of grace, that we may obtain mercy" (Hebrews 4:16). Jesus, as our great High Priest, has entered into heaven for us, making the door open to each of us to have direct entrance to God. "There is one God, and one mediator between God and men, the man Christ Jesus" (1 Timothy 2:5).

---

*The true shepherd of God is one who*
*gives himself for the flock, not one who is*
*demanding that the flock give*
*themselves to him.*

---

For any other person to take that position or role is scripturally *wrong*. The doctrine of the Nicolaitanes would put a man between you and God, and that is always wrong. God will deal with you directly, personally, and individually—and wants to deal with you directly, personally, and individually.

God will listen to you just as rapidly as He'll listen to me. God loves you just as much as He loves Billy Graham. He's just as concerned about you as He is anybody else. You have, through Jesus Christ, this glorious access to come directly to God. God will guide you, and God will show you His path and His way.

### What Did Jesus Say?

In Mark 10 we find that James and John were seeking to establish something of an eldership:

> And James and John, the sons of Zebedee, come unto him, saying, Master, we would that thou shouldest do for us whatsoever we shall desire. And he said unto them, What would ye that I should do for you? They said unto him,

Grant unto us that we may sit, one on thy right
hand, and the other on thy left hand, in thy
glory. But Jesus said unto them, Ye know not
what ye ask: can ye drink of the cup that I
drink of? and be baptized with the baptism
that I am baptized with? And they said unto
him, We can. And Jesus said unto them, Ye
shall indeed drink of the cup that I drink of;
and with the baptism that I am baptized
withal shall ye be baptized: but to sit on my
right hand and on my left hand is not mine to
give; but it shall be given to them for whom it
is prepared. And when the ten heard it, they
began to be much displeased with James and
John (Mark 10:35–41).

Jesus called them to him and said, "Ye know that they
which are accounted to rule over the Gentiles exercise
lordship over them (that same Greek word as in 1 Peter
5:3, "to bring into submission, to exercise authority over");
and their great ones exercise authority upon them." Notice
what Jesus said in Mark 10:43: **"But so shall it not be
among you."** There is not to be the establishing of
authority or the exercising of lordship.

Whosoever will be great among you, shall be
your minister: and whosoever of you will be the
chiefest, shall be servant of all. For even the
Son of man came not to be ministered unto, but to
minister, and to give his life a ransom for many
(Mark 10:43–45).

Jesus didn't come to be ministered to but, rather, to
minister and to give Himself. Thus, He is the True
Shepherd. "I am the true shepherd and I give my life for my
sheep." The true shepherd is one who gives himself for the
flock, not one who is demanding that the flock give

themselves to him. He is more interested in feeding the flock than fleecing the flock.

I think the most familiar passage in the Bible, outside of John 3:16, has the answer. David said:

> The LORD is my shepherd; I shall not want. He maketh me to lie down in green pastures: he leadeth me beside the still waters. He restoreth my soul: he leadeth me in the paths of righteousness for his name's sake (Psalm 23:1–3).

If you can have the Lord as your Shepherd, I don't know why you would want to settle for anything less. If David, under the old economy, could have the Lord as his Shepherd, how much more under the new relationship through Jesus Christ can we know and submit ourselves to the authority of God within our lives.

I would urge you to submit yourself to the authority of Jesus Christ. Submit yourself to the authority of God's Word. Realize that you're responsible to God. Every man must give an account of himself unto God (Romans 14:12). Learn to go to God for all your needs, for all your decisions, and for the guidance for your life. God is faithful. He will lead you and guide you.

### Christian "Possession"

The question has been forced upon us: "Can a born-again Christian be possessed by a demon?" The answer based on the Scriptures and on logic is an unequivocal *no!*

The proponents of this unscriptural doctrine use such terms as Christians being "invaded by demons" rather than demon possessed. This is nothing more than a word game and a smoke screen to hide the scriptural weakness of their position.

They also present an illogical supposition that demons can invade or control the mind or body but not the spirit. God's Word declares that the body is a temple of the Holy Ghost who is in us. We're told to glorify God in our bodies and in our spirits, which are His (1 Corinthians 6:19, 20). In 2 Corinthians 6:14–16 the question is asked:

> What communion hath light with darkness? And what concord hath Christ with Belial... And what agreement hath the temple of God with idols? for ye are the temple of the living God; as God hath said, I will dwell in them.

To say that a Christian's body or mind can be possessed or invaded by demons is to contradict the Word of God and declare a communion of light and darkness, that God and Satan are dwelling together.

The Scriptures also teach us that Christ is seated in the heavenlies, far above all principalities and powers and mights and dominions (Ephesians 1:21, 22). These are references to spirit beings—and Christ is far above them. Where am I as a believer? According to Ephesians 2:6, I am seated together with Christ in the heavenlies. As Christians we're in a warfare against these principalities and powers (Ephesians 6:12). We need the help of God to stand, for these rulers of the darkness can and do attack us in a variety of ways. But they cannot come in and take control of our lives.

The Scriptures also teach that we are in Christ, and that He is in us (John 14:20). It is Christ in us which is our hope of glory (Colossians 1:27). Christ said concerning Satan, "The prince of this world cometh, and hath nothing in me"

(John 14:30). If I'm in Christ and Satan has nothing in Him, Satan can have nothing in me—praise the Lord!

We also read in 1 John 5:18,

> We know that whosoever is born of God sinneth not; but he that is begotten of God keepeth himself, and that wicked one toucheth him not.

What about these experiences of Christians having demons cast out of them? What are the voices that name themselves, the writhing on the floor, and the regurgitation? I don't know. I'm thankful that, since I don't engage in these unscriptural practices, I don't have to explain them.

Some of the names given by these supposed demons which are more popular are lust, hatred, liar, gluttony, envy, fear, and jealousy. These things are classified in Galatians 5:19–21 as the works of the flesh. We're told to "put off all these" (Colossians 3:8), or by the Spirit to "mortify the deeds of the body" (Romans 8:13; 6:3–14). Not once are we commanded to have them cast out.

It seems to me that this whole Christian-and-demon trip is a cop-out for the flesh. I would like to find some easy way to get rid of my fleshly nature, and rather than the painful process of crucifixion, I'd just like to have it cast out. It's also a way of escaping the responsibility for my fleshly actions. How can I be blamed if "the devil made me do it"?

There doesn't exist one piece of evidence in the Scriptures that Jesus Christ, His apostles, or the early church once sought to cast demons of the flesh out of anyone in the Body of Christ. The works of the flesh were recognized, and we're instructed in how to deal with them. Never are we taught that they're to be exorcised.

Even in the supposed cases from the Scriptures which would confirm that demons could inhabit a Christian— such as Ananias and Sapphira, "Why hath Satan filled thine heart..." (Acts 5:3), or Simon the sorcerer, "Thou art in the gall of bitterness, and in the bond of iniquity" (Acts 8:23)—Peter didn't practice exorcism. Instead, there was instant judgment of death in the first case and a call to repentance in the other.

It is sad that many Christians and non-Christians seem to have a greater interest in Satan and being possessed by demons than they do in Christ and being possessed by His Holy Spirit. Those who fall into the practices of exorcism soon seem to be looking for and placing a greater emphasis on the power of Satan to attack than on the power of Christ to keep. Demons become the center of their conversations and teachings rather than Jesus Christ.

We can rejoice in God's Word, "Greater is he that is in you, than he that is in the world" (1 John 4:4). Thanks be to God who gives us the victory through Jesus Christ our Lord! We as Christians are told in James 4:7 to "resist," not "cast out," the devil—and he will flee from us.

### Three Things in Common

There are three interesting similarities in these two false doctrines:

1. Both doctrines have really divided the body of Christ across the United States.

2. They both have sterilizing effects. If you become so involved in casting demons out of yourself, every time you

gather together with the local body the whole emphasis is upon demons rather than upon the Lord. Soon, you become so inward that you're no longer effective in your witness for Jesus Christ. You're too preoccupied about some demon activity within your life.

The doctrine of shepherding is also sterilizing in its effects. Since you become spiritually responsible for everyone and anyone you lead to Christ, you shouldn't lead anyone to Christ until you're spiritually mature enough to accept that responsibility.

3. Both false doctrines appeal to people who are seeking to escape the responsibility of their own actions. This is where these doctrines actually have their appeal.

"It wasn't really *me!* A *demon* was responsible for that outburst of temper. A *demon* was responsible for that moment of lustful passion." It's throwing the responsibility for my actions over onto the demons, rather than accepting it as part of my old rotten flesh.

The shepherding doctrine relieves me of the obligation and responsibility of my conduct. "I don't have to be responsible for what I do. The shepherd tells me what to do." Thus, he is the one who is responsible for my actions—whether they're right or wrong, in the will of God or not. And I escape responsibility for my own deeds.

There are many people who don't want to be responsible for the things they do. Both of these false doctrines offer that escape from, and of, responsibility.

# CHAPTER 8

# THE RAPTURE!

Death to the Christian is so different than to the non-Christian that it's incorrect even to use the same term. For the Christian death is really a *transition*.

Paul said, "For me to live is Christ, and to die is gain... I am in a strait betwixt two, having a desire to depart, and to be with Christ; which is far better" (Philippians 1:21, 23). Paul said that we who are in this body do groan, earnestly desiring to be delivered; not that we would be unclothed but that we might be clothed with that body which is from heaven (2 Corinthians 5:2).

Speaking to the Thessalonians concerning their loved ones who had already died in Christ, Paul said,

> I would not have you to be ignorant, brethren, concerning them which are asleep, that ye sorrow not, even as others which have no hope. For if we believe that Jesus died and rose again, even so them also which sleep in Jesus will God bring with him. For this we say unto you by the word of the Lord, that we which are alive and remain unto the coming of the Lord shall not [precede] them which are asleep. For the Lord himself shall descend from

> heaven with a shout, with the voice of the
> archangel, and with the trump of God: and the
> dead in Christ shall rise first: **Then we which
> are alive and remain shall be caught up
> together with them in the clouds, to meet the
> Lord in the air:** and so shall we ever be with
> the Lord. Wherefore comfort one another with
> these words (1 Thessalonians 4:13–18, emphasis
> added).

Some people would ridicule the idea or concept of the Rapture of the church. They declare that the word "rapture" isn't even found in the Bible. It all depends on which Bible you're reading. The phrase "caught up" in 1 Thessalonians 4:17 is the Greek word *harpazo*, which actually means "to be snatched away violently." The Latin equivalent of *harpazo* is the verb *rapio*, "to take away by force." In the Latin Vulgate, one of the oldest Bibles in existence, the appropriate tense of *rapio* appears in verse 17. *Raptus* is the past participle of *rapio*. Our English words "rapt" and "rapture" stem from this past participle. Although "rapture" isn't in the King James Bible, the basic word does appear in the Latin Vulgate.

### What Is Meant by the Rapture?

The Rapture refers to that event where Jesus Christ snatches His church out of this world. It shall happen suddenly without any notice. The Rapture of the church and the Second Coming of Jesus Christ are completely different. At the Rapture, Jesus is coming for His saints.

In 1 Corinthians 15:51–52 Paul said, "Behold, I show you a mystery; We shall not all sleep, but we shall all be changed [metamorphosis, a change of body], In a moment, in the twinkling of an eye." You won't even realize it's happened until it's all over. Suddenly, you're in the presence of the Lord with all the church!

We, the church, will be changed. Paul wrote to the Philippians,

> For our [citizenship] is in heaven; from whence also we look for the Savior, the Lord Jesus Christ: Who shall change our vile body, that it may be fashioned like unto his glorious [image] (Philippians 3:20–21).

Describing the metamorphosis Paul wrote to Corinth, "For this corruptible must put on incorruption, and this mortal must put on immortality" (1 Corinthians 15:53). At the Second Coming we will return with Jesus Christ. Jude 14 tells us, "Behold, the Lord cometh with ten thousands of his saints."

### When Will the Rapture Take Place?

Jesus said, "No man knows the day or hour..." For us to presume to declare some date or some hour would be an unscriptural presumption. If we say we know the hour, we're boasting of knowledge superior to Christ's when He was upon the earth.

Although we do not know the exact time of the Rapture, in 1 Thessalonians 5 Paul said,

> But of the times and seasons, brethren, ye have no need that I write unto you. For yourselves know perfectly that the day of the Lord so cometh as a thief in the night. For when they shall say, Peace and safety; then sudden destruction cometh...**But ye, brethren, are not in darkness, that that day should overtake you as a thief** (emphasis added).

The Bible is saying that the Rapture shouldn't come to you as a surprise.

### Why Should "That Day" Not Overtake Us as a Thief?

God has given to us the warnings that would precede the coming of Jesus Christ. One of the greatest signs to the world today is the reestablishment of the nation Israel. For years Bible scholars had looked forward to the regathering of the nation Israel based on many Scriptures (including Matthew 24:32), and applying expositional constancy (fig tree or figs in parables symbolize the nation Israel). Skeptics ridiculed this prophecy. Never in history had a nation been born out of the past, but a miracle has taken place and a nation has been reborn. God has reestablished Israel among the family of nations on the earth. God has fulfilled His promise even as He said He would.

Psalm 102:16 declares, "When the Lord shall build up Zion, he shall appear in his glory." Because the Lord is building up Zion, the orthodox Jew today is looking for his Messiah. We are too! We're looking forward to this fulfillment of God's promise—the coming again of our great God and Savior Jesus Christ.

> Now learn a parable of the fig tree; When his branch is yet tender, and putteth forth leaves, ye know that summer is nigh:...know that it [His coming] is near, even at the doors. Verily I say unto you, This generation shall not pass, till all these things be fulfilled (Matthew 24:32–34).

### What "Generation"?

Not the generation Christ was talking to, because they've passed—but the generation that saw the fig tree budding forth. The coming of Jesus Christ is "even at the doors." The rebirth of Israel should be a sign to every child of God!

Jesus said throughout the rest of Matthew 24, "Watch... be ye also ready." That was the constant warning to the church: watch and be ready. In Luke 21:28 when Jesus was speaking of these same things, using again the parable of the fig tree, He said, "And when these things begin to come to pass, then look up, and lift up your heads; for your redemption draweth nigh."

### Will the Rapture Precede the Great Tribulation?

There are arguments and Scriptures that people can present for pre-, mid-, and post-Tribulation theories. My personal opinion is that Jesus will come before the Great Tribulation to rapture His church. I don't believe that the church will go through the Great Tribulation period.

In 1 Thessalonians 5:9 Paul wrote, "For God hath not appointed us to wrath, but to obtain salvation by our Lord Jesus Christ." Paul said the same in Romans 5:9—we've not been appointed to wrath. Jesus, in the whole context of the Tribulation, said, "Pray always, that ye may be accounted worthy to escape all these things that shall come to pass, and to stand before the Son of Man" (Luke 21:36). My prayer is that I will be accounted worthy to escape all of these things that are going to come to pass upon the earth.

The Lord divided the Book of Revelation into three sections: [1] "Write the things which thou hast seen, [2] and the things which are, [3] and the things which shall be hereafter [meta tauta]" (Revelation 1:19). John, in obedience to the commandment, wrote in chapter 1 the vision of Christ that he saw on the island of Patmos. In chapters 2 and 3 he wrote of the church and the message of Jesus to the seven churches. Let's look at two of these messages where Jesus made reference to His coming again.

1. The church of Thyatira had introduced the worship of idols within the church. Jesus said,

> I have a few things against thee, because thou sufferest that woman Jezebel... to seduce my servants to commit fornication... I gave her space to repent of her fornication; and she repented not. Behold, I will cast her into a bed, and them that commit adultery with her into **great tribulation, except they repent of their** deeds (Revelation 2:20–22, emphasis added).

The unrepentant church of Thyatira, which had gone into spiritual "fornication" (idolatry and saint worship), was to be cast into the Great Tribulation unless, the Lord said, she repented.

2. To the church of Philadelphia in Revelation 3:10 Jesus said, "Because thou hast kept the word of my patience, I also will **keep thee from the hour of temptation,** which shall come...to try them that dwell upon the earth" (emphasis added). The Rapture can happen at any moment—and it's exciting to realize that as a Christian you may never finish reading this article! After the close of the messages to the churches, Revelation 4:1 begins and ends with the Greek phrase *meta tauta*. "After these things," John said, "...behold, a door was opened in heaven: and the first voice which I heard was a trumpet talking with me, which said, Come up hither, and I will show thee things which must be **after these things** [meta tauta]" (emphasis added).

## After What "Things"?

Jesus spoke of church things in chapters 2 and 3. These must be the things that will take place after the church is taken out of the earth. I believe that 4:1 of the Book of Revelation is the place of the Rapture of the church. That "voice" in heaven and "trumpet" are the same as in 1 Thessalonians 4:16. With the trump of God and the archangel saying, "Come up hither," we, the church, will be gathered together with the Lord in the heavens.

## What Happens After Revelation 4:1?

John describes the heavenly scene in chapter 4. In chapter 5 he saw the scroll with seven seals in the right hand of Him who is sitting upon the throne. An angel proclaimed with a loud voice, "Who is worthy to open the book, and to loose the seals?" John began to sob convulsively because no one in heaven or earth, nor under the earth was found worthy to even look upon the scroll (Revelation 5:2–4).

Then one of the elders said, "Weep not: behold, the Lion of the tribe of Judah, the Root of David, hath prevailed to open the book and to loose the seven seals." John turned and saw Jesus as a Lamb that had been slain, "...and he came and took the book out of the right hand of him that sat upon the throne." Immediately, they brought forth the "...vials full of [incense] which are the prayers of saints. And they sung a new song, saying, Thou art worthy to take the book, and to open the seals thereof; for thou wast slain, and hast redeemed us to God by thy blood out of every kindred, and tongue, and people, and nation; and hast made us unto our God kings and priests: and we shall reign on the earth" (Revelation 5:5–10). Notice the song that is being sung.

## *Who Can Sing That Song?*

It's not the song of Israel and the covenant relationship with God. People from all the families of the earth, not just one family of Abraham, are singing. It's a people who have been redeemed by the blood of Jesus Christ. Only the church can sing that song.

In Revelation 5:11 after Jesus takes the scroll, John said that innumerable multitudes, "ten thousand times ten thousands" worship the Lamb, declaring His worthiness to receive the honor, the authority, and the glory. In Revelation 6, Jesus proceeds to loose the seals of the scrolls. With the very first seal there comes forth the white horse rider, "...conquering, and to conquer." This, I believe, is the entrance of the Antichrist because he's followed by wars, death, famine, and desolation. Certainly, the Second Coming of Christ isn't going to be followed by such events, but by the glorious establishment of the Kingdom.

## *Now, Where's the Church?*

Before the Tribulation ever begins the church is in heaven singing and praising the Lord for His worthiness to take the scroll and loose the seals. The Tribulation doesn't start until the seven seals begin to be broken.

## *Then Why All the Confusion Concerning Pre-Trib, Mid-Trib, and Post-Trib Rapture?*

In Revelation 13:7, reference is made to the beast, "...making war with the saints," and he is given power to overcome them during the middle of the Tribulation period. Jesus in Matthew 24:29–31 said about His Second Coming,

> Immediately after the tribulation of those
> days... they shall see the Son of man coming in

> the clouds of heaven with power and great
> glory. And he shall send his angels with a
> great sound of a trumpet, and they shall gather
> together his elect from the four winds, from one
> end of heaven to the other.

By defining "the saints" and "His elect" as being the
church you would have the church in the Tribulation
period. I believe "His elect" is a reference to the nation
Israel, if you read it in context.

Christ said, "Pray ye that your flight be not in the
winter, neither on the Sabbath day..." when fleeing out of
Jerusalem (Matthew 24:16–20). How many in the church
expect to be in Jerusalem fleeing when the Antichrist sets
up his image within the temple? How many of you would
be praying, "O God, don't let it be on the Sabbath day"?
The church doesn't keep the Sabbath day; that's God's
covenant relationship with Israel. The fact is that Israel is
"His elect." He's going to gather them back into their land
for the Kingdom Age at His return.

As Paul said in Romans 11:25–26,

> ...that blindness in part [has] happened to
> Israel, until the fullness of the Gentiles be come
> in. And so all Israel shall be saved: as it is
> written, There shall come out of Zion the
> Deliverer, and shall turn away ungodliness
> from Jacob.

"The saints" of Revelation 13:7 are also the same. They
are God's nation Israel which He has now established
again in a priority basis upon the earth during this last
seven-year Tribulation period.

The mistake and the confusion regarding the church's
place in the last times arise out of a misunderstanding of

God's full prophecies concerning the nation Israel. Israel will be going through the Great Tribulation. This will be the time of Jacob's troubles spoken of in Scripture (Jeremiah 30:7). This will be the time when, as even Jesus said, "Ye shall not see me henceforth, till ye shall say, Blessed is he that cometh in the name of the Lord" (Matthew 23:39). After the Great Tribulation period Israel will be saying, "O, blessed is He who comes in the name of the Lord!" Jesus shall return again with His church at the Second Coming of Christ.

Zechariah the prophet said, "And one shall say unto him; What are these wounds in your hands? Then he shall answer; Those with which I was wounded in the house of my friends" (Zechariah 13:6). Thus, the glorious first recognition of Jesus as Israel's Messiah when He comes the second time with the church to establish His reign upon the earth.

### What Should I Do as a Christian?

In the light of the fact that the Lord might come even today, there are certain things we should do. But first, let me tell you what you shouldn't do. Don't quit your job, sell your house, or see how much money you can borrow figuring you won't have to pay it back. Jesus said, "Occupy until I come" (Luke 19:13). He intends for us to go right on in our work.

Jesus said, "Watch" (Matthew 24:42). You should be watching. In Hebrews it says, "And unto them that look for him shall he appear the second time..." (Hebrews 9:28). You should be ready. Jesus said, "Therefore be ye also ready; for in such an hour as you think not the Son of man cometh" (Matthew 24:44). Amos cried out, "Prepare to meet thy God" (Amos 4:12). You need to prepare. That preparation is in giving your heart and life to Jesus Christ, receiving His forgiveness and the blotting out of your sins and transgressions. And then wait. James said, "Be patient therefore, brethren, unto the coming of the Lord. Behold, the husbandman waiteth...Be ye also patient; establish your hearts" (James 5:7–8). In 2 Peter 3:3–4 we learn that in the last days there will be scoffers that will come and say, "Where is the promise of his coming?" But God "is not slack concerning his promise, as some men count slackness; but is longsuffering to us" (v. 9).

### The Question at This Point Is, "Are You Ready?"

Consider the Lord proclaiming today, "This is the end for the church! You have finished your witness. Come home!" Would you be gathered with the church to meet the Lord in the air, or would you be down here scratching your head wondering what's going on?

How much better to go with the church than to be left behind to face the Tribulation and all the horror coming upon the earth. Why make it tough for yourself when the Lord wants to make it easy on you? Why not just open your heart and life to Jesus Christ now? Why not just receive Him as your Lord and Savior and, as He said, be ready. What do you need to be ready? Jesus Christ dwelling in your heart and in your life.

### What About Those Who Miss?

At times there may be a hesitancy in our hearts concerning the coming of Jesus Christ because of what will happen to our unsaved family members when He returns.

Once we've been caught up, many of our loved ones, who have been hassled by our witness and upset with our testimony, will realize that they've actually missed the opportunity of being raptured with the church. As a result, they'll become dead serious with God and will choose to be martyred during the Great Tribulation period by refusing to take the mark of the beast. They will choose death in preference to the mark and, thus, will be saved (Revelation 20:4).

In Revelation 7:9–14, John saw in heaven "a great multitude, which no man could number, of all nations, and kindreds...clothed with white robes..." singing of salvation. The elder said to John, "These are they which came out of **great tribulation,** and have washed their robes, and made them white in the blood of the Lamb" (emphasis added). In Revelation 6:9–11 under the fifth seal, these souls martyred during the Tribulation period are waiting for their opportunity to enter the heavenly scene. They are told to wait a little longer until the total number be slain as they were slain.

Being a Tribulation saint is a hard way to come. As Jesus said, "For then shall be great tribulation..." such as the world never has seen before or ever will see again (Matthew 24:21). *Why wait?* Why slough off your chances of being in the glorious excitement of being with the Lord when He catches up the church?

# WHAT DOES GOD REQUIRE OF ME?

David said in Psalm 19:

> The heavens declare the glory of God; and the firmament showeth his handiwork. Day unto day uttereth speech, and night unto night showeth knowledge. There is no speech nor language, where their voice is not heard (v. 1–3).

God has made Himself known in nature. I have become conscious and aware of the fact of God's existence. All around me there is a witness. The voice of God is speaking to me and telling me of the *fact* of God—and it cannot be denied.

Recently, as I was looking through volume "E" of the encyclopedia, I started reading about the eye. I became fascinated with the facets of the human eye: the muscles that control the movements, the methods by which the pictures are taken at 18 impulses per second, and impressed upon this vitreous jelly substance, vibrating the message into the brain so that the brain distinguishes images and the color. I was amazed at the intricate nature and the complexities of the human eye. I was just overwhelmed!

The description of the human eye spoke to me about the wisdom and creative genius God has exercised in creating this human body. For me to think that the eye "just happened" is impossible. Its incredible design and function gave me a very powerful testimony of the fact that God *does* exist—the fact that God made me, using infinite wisdom in the creation of the human body.

Man becomes conscious of God through the universe about him because "Day unto day uttereth speech, and night unto night showeth knowledge. There is no speech nor language, where their voice is not heard" (Psalm 19:2). The universe speaks to us of the fact of God's existence. But once I become conscious of the fact that God does exist, make that acknowledgment, and realize that God has created me as the highest order of His created beings that I can observe, then I begin to wonder about the *purpose* of creation.

"God, if You have created me above the animal kingdom, if You have created me with these capacities and these abilities that I possess, *why* did You create me?" What is God's purpose in creation? More specifically, what is the purpose for my life? Do I die like a dog to rot as a log? Or did God have a real reason when He formed man out of the dust of the earth, breathed into him the breath of God, and man became a living soul?

## *What Does God Require of Me?*

Why did He create me? These questions become of primary concern and interest. Does life have a meaning or not? Is there a purpose for being or not? Is there a reason behind it all? Why does life seem to be so empty and unfulfilled?

Psychologists tell us that the neurotic problems of man begin with a basic *frustration*—that awareness, that inner consciousness that there must be something more to life than what he has yet experienced. Every man is conscious of an emptiness within his life. There must be a reason for living beyond what he has already discovered. There must be something more than just this! Like the song, "Is that all there is?"—or is there more?

In searching for the answer, I turn to the Word of God. It declares that God definitely does have a plan and a purpose for my life. God created me with a design and with a purpose in His mind. I'm not here by accident. My life isn't a "fortuitous concurrence of accidental circumstances." God has His hand on it all the way along. God has a reason, a plan, and a purpose for not only my life but for your life as an individual, for not only the overall population and mankind in general but for individuals as well. God has a plan and a purpose for you, and He created you with that plan and purpose in mind.

The greatest and the busiest life apart from God is empty. To try to live apart from God's plan is utter futility. King Solomon lived a satiated life. He describes it in Ecclesiastes 2:10, "Whatsoever mine eyes desired I kept not from them." He did absolutely everything that came into his heart and mind. He glutted himself, looking for something that would be fulfilling, that would meet that deep, inner need.

Solomon indulged himself with life. He sought for wisdom and applied himself until he became the wisest man who ever lived. But fulfillment didn't lie there. So he indulged himself with pleasure—but it wasn't there either. Then he began to pursue great works and possessions. He began to build monuments after his name—but fulfillment wasn't there. Then he sought it in wealth, but it wasn't there. He sought it in sex, but it wasn't there. After satiating himself with all these things—no fulfillment! He finally came to the conclusion, "Emptiness, emptiness, always emptiness, and vexation of spirit." He said, "I hate life." *It was empty!*

---

*For my own good, for my own well being,*
*for my own sake of sanity, I must discover*
*God's plan and purpose for my life.*

---

If you leave God out of your life, you're destined to end up with an emptiness within that cannot be filled by anything. You can try to fulfill yourself with other things, but they'll never fill the real need within your life. For my own good, for my own well-being, for my own sake of sanity, I must discover God's plan and God's purpose for my life. What does God want of me? Why did God make me? What does God require of me?

### Ideal Requirement

In Deuteronomy 18:13 we find that God requires this of me: Moses, in making a summation of the law, the commandments and the judgments of God, declared, "Thou shalt be perfect with the Lord thy God." What does

God require of you? *Perfection.* Jesus said the same thing, "Be ye therefore perfect, even as your Father which is in heaven is perfect" (Matthew 5:48).

What does it mean to be "perfect"? Let me ask you this: "What does it mean to be imperfect?" I understand that much better. The root word of sin means "missing the mark." The root word of *perfection* comes from "hitting the mark." To be perfect means to absolutely hit the mark, to be exactly what God wants you to be.

When I read in the Scriptures that God requires me to be "perfect" with the Lord my God, I immediately realize that I have failed. Standing in the consciousness of the ideal of Jesus Christ, I'm aware of the fact that I'm a sinner. I've missed the mark!

---

*God requires that I be "perfect."*
*Immediately, I realize that I've missed*
*the mark. I'm a sinner. What do I do now?*

---

When I stand with my fellowman, I get a different consciousness. I say, "I know I'm not perfect, but at least I'm not like they are!" I can always find someone whose face is a little dirtier than mine, and I take comfort in that fact. "I know mine isn't clean, but did you see how dirty his is!" We look at our lives the same way. "I know I'm not totally clean, but at least I'm not as dirty as someone else!"

Jesus said that in measuring yourself by men you do err (Luke 18:9–14). I must measure myself by the ideal in Jesus Christ, because if I want to know *why* God created man, if I want to know the *purpose* of the creation of man, I cannot look around and find it. I must look to *Jesus Christ*, for in Him I find God's ideal fulfilled. In Christ I find what God intended when He made man and placed him on the Earth.

So, as I look at Jesus Christ and stand in His presence, the presence of this ideal, I realize and must confess that I'm a sinner. I've missed the mark. Even when I wanted to hit it and did all in my power to hit it, I still missed. I've failed God. I'm a sinner. I realize that immediately. I've failed in fulfilling the purpose of God for man. Is there any hope for me? Is there any chance for me—a sinful, failing man?

The word *gospel* means "good news." The Scripture says that the disciples went everywhere preaching the good news. What "good news"? The good news that there is help, there is hope—the good news of God's love for sinning, failing, rebellious man who is missing the mark. The *good news* is that "God so loved the world, that he gave his only begotten Son, that whosoever believeth in him should not perish, but have everlasting life" (John 3:16).

God's ideal requirement for me is that I be *perfect*. I've failed. What about me now? What does God require of me now?

A man came to Jesus one day and asked, "What shall we do, that we might work the works of God?" (John 6:28). This is a question of perennial interest.

God's good news is that He has provided for our failure. God has accepted the responsibility of the guilt of my sin and my weaknesses. Jesus Christ took upon Himself my penalty—all my sin and all my missing of the mark. "All we like sheep have gone astray; we have turned every one to his own way; and the Lord hath laid on him the iniquity of us all" (Isaiah 53:6). Jesus, taking my sin upon Himself, died in my place. God was in Christ reconciling the world to Himself. God provided for my failure, for my sin.

## What Must I Do to Do the Works of God?

Jesus said, "This is the work of God, that ye believe on him whom he hath sent" (John 6:29). That's simple enough, isn't it? God required perfection—I missed. What does He now require of me, the imperfect creature that I am? He requires that I just believe on His provision of love in Jesus Christ and that I accept Jesus Christ as my Lord and Savior. This is the work of God: that you believe on Him whom He has sent. It's so easy that anyone can do it. "You mean I can do it right now?" You bet you can!

When I believe in Jesus Christ—accepting Him as my personal Lord and Savior, realizing that He took my sin and my failures upon Himself and died for me, that redemption covers me as a personal individual, and I say, "O Jesus, I believe and accept and take You now as my Lord and Savior"—what happens? Jesus comes into my life with a vital power. The Scripture says,

> As many as received him, to them gave he
> power to become the sons of God, even to them
> that believe on his name (John 1:12).

Jesus comes into my life with power—a new dynamic, a new force. This new power begins to change me. He takes away my old nature bent toward sin and constantly missing the mark, and He gives me, instead, His new nature. He declared of Himself, "I do always those things that please him [the Father]" (John 8:29).

Jesus Christ gives me the nature that helps me do those things that are pleasing to the Father—those things I couldn't do because of the weakness of my flesh, as I'm just a miserable failure. Christ now begins to give me the power to make those necessary changes so I can start hitting the mark even as God desires that I do.

---

*God requires that I just believe on His*
*provision of love in Jesus Christ—*
*accepting Him as my personal Lord and*
*Savior!*

---

If any man be in Christ, he is a new creature:
old things are passed away; behold, all things
are become new (2 Corinthians 5:17).

Jesus imparts to me that new nature by which I can now become perfect and hit the mark!

Now, I have no intention of giving you the false concept that I'm saying, "I'm perfect." Far from it! Every time I say, "Lord, there's nothing to this one. Let me show You I can hit the mark," I miss it. Every time I try in myself and I'm not yielding to those forces of His Spirit within, I still miss the mark—and I'm still stupid enough to keep trying in my own self. But I've found that every time I yield to the power and dynamic of His Spirit within my life, He puts me right on target. I can hit it with His power and help as He dwells within me. His nature is fulfilled within me and I become more and more like Jesus Christ.

Paul the apostle, writing 30 years after his conversion on the Damascus Road, said, "Not as though I had already attained, either were already perfect" (Philippians 3:12). This great saint is saying, "I'm not yet perfect. I'm still missing. Not as much—praise God for that!" There are those glorious times when I yield and I'm hitting the bull's-eye. God is teaching me the lessons day by day of my absolute need for Him and the absolute necessity of turning everything over to Him. God's ideal is being fulfilled in me through the power of Jesus Christ. My failures are now taken care of. I'm on the right path. By holding on to the hand of Jesus and receiving His power and strength, He is guiding me. Along with Paul, I'm pressing towards the mark for the prize of the high calling of God which is in Christ Jesus (Philippians 3:14).

"Be ye therefore perfect." Don't let that discourage you. Of course you can't be perfect! But yield yourself to those forces which will give you that new nature in Jesus Christ, enabling you to fulfill God's ideal requirement. God hasn't given up on His ideal requirement. As I hold on to the hand of Jesus Christ, one of these days I'll be standing right in the presence of God, the One who created the whole universe.

As God looks at me with His searching eyes from which nothing is hidden, I'll stand there in the bare nakedness of my being—but, praise God, He's going to see me in Christ absolutely perfect!

Why? Not because Chuck Smith is perfect, but because Jesus is able to keep me from falling and to present me faultless before the presence of His glory with exceeding joy (Jude 24). If you believe on Jesus Christ and yield to the power of His Spirit within your life, one day He'll present you faultless before the throne of God.

If you believe and trust in Him, the work of God is already at work in your life helping you to hit the mark that He has set. If not, salvation is very simple. All you have to do is say, "Lord, I know I've failed, but take over and help me. Lord, I turn it over to You." If you within your heart at this moment will do that, then He'll take over. He's just waiting.

Jesus said, "Behold, I stand at the door, and knock: if any man hear my voice, and open the door, I will come in" (Revelation 3:20). He's standing at your heart's door right now. He's knocking. He's waiting. Will you open it? As the Spirit of God is speaking to your heart, will you say, "Okay, Lord, I give up. Take over. Make me what You want me to be." It's just that easy. Won't you do it now?

You don't have to go forward at an altar call. You don't have to be singing. All you have to do is decide within your heart, "Lord, I turn it over to You." And He will give you that power to become a child of God.

### Secret of Strength

Years ago, I taught my two boys how to use a bow. When I first taught them I bought 25-pound bows—bigger than they were actually capable of handling in the beginning, but I wanted them to learn with a powerful bow. So, as I took each boy out to teach him how to use a bow and arrow, I'd first show him the proper grip. I said, "Take hold of the bow with your left hand," and I'd stand behind him. As he held the bow, I took a firm hold of his left wrist.

Then I reached around him and said, "Take the draw string with your two fingers, notch the arrow, and begin to draw it back." I took hold of his right wrist and began to draw back, holding both his wrists with my hands so that, when the bow had been drawn, we were able to hold it there and sight the target. Then I said, "Release!"—and he'd release his fingers.

Actually, my boys were able to draw that bow only because I had hold of their wrists. Their hands were made strong, really, by the fact that their father was holding on to their wrists and drawing for them.

When God's hand is upon you, you are strong. When God's hand is upon you, you're able to face any situation. "If God be for us, who can be against us?" (Romans 8:31). With God's help I am sufficient—no matter what the trial or the testing or the problem may be. When God's hand is upon my life, I am strengthened and strong enough to meet any obstacle. That is always the secret of strength!

# CHAPTER 10

*Your life is an open book!*

# BE AN EXAMPLE

Be thou an example of the believers, in word, in conversation, in charity, in spirit, in faith, in purity. Till I come, give attendance to reading, to exhortation, to doctrine. Neglect not the gift that is in thee, which was given thee by prophecy, with the laying on of the hands of the presbytery. Meditate upon these things; give thyself wholly to them; that thy profiting may appear to all. Take heed unto thyself, and unto the doctrine; continue in them: for in doing this thou shalt both save thyself, and them that hear thee (1 Timothy 4:12–16).

As a Christian, you're a marked person because you have claimed to be a child of God. People are watching you to find out what a child of God is like. How does he react under pressure? What does he do when the going gets rough? What does he do when there seems to be no way out?

At work, at school, in your neighborhood, people are watching you. They are watching you, because they have problems and they want answers to their problems. Christianity promises an answer. You're a Christian, so they want to see if the answer works.

Whether you want to be or not, you're an example of a believer to those people around you. They're watching you, because they don't know what a believer is all about. They assume that you're what a believer should be.

Being a Christian is a glorious thrill! God has washed away my sins and written my name in the Book of Life. It is also a fantastic responsibility. People are watching me to find out what a Christian looks like, what he acts like, and what he is.

Many people will never read a Bible, but they're going to read your life like a book. They'll be watching every chapter to see what it says. Be thou an example, not to the believers, but of the believers. By the way you're living, people are determining whether or not they want to believe in Jesus Christ. Is your life drawing people to Him, or are they walking away from Him, saying, "Well, I thought maybe Christianity had the answer, but I guess maybe it doesn't."

*What are the areas that people are scrutinizing and studying in you?* First of all, your words, the things that you say. Jesus said, "Out of the abundance of the heart the mouth speaketh" (Matthew 12:34). Your words reveal what you are, what you're thinking, what is down inside. It's not only what you say but, so many times, how you say it.

How many times have we said things that we'd like to retract immediately? "Oh no! That's not what I meant!" We'd like to say it again in a nicer way, without that cutting harshness with which we spoke. It's not what I say in front of a congregation that counts so much, it's what I say to my family when we're within the four walls of our home, or the things I say when I'm by myself and think no one else is listening.

Another thing people are observing is how you conduct yourself. If you can whistle and be happy when everything is great...so what? A heathen can, too! People aren't watching your conduct so much when things are going good. They're watching your conduct when things are tough. They want to see how you react in adversity. When it seems that everything is pressing in and things are getting very difficult, then can you smile?

You shouldn't be one thing at church and another thing at business. You should conduct your business as a Christian. If you're working for an employer, you should give him a full day's work for the wage that he's paying you. He's watching your conduct. Are you taking a lot of time standing and visiting with others on the employer's time? He's making note of it. If you take longer on the coffee breaks and more trips to the washroom than anybody else, it makes a poor witness.

You say: "There's this guy at work. He's so ripe! He's so ready to accept Jesus Christ!" But if you're spending the boss's time witnessing to this guy about the Lord, it isn't right. You may say, "I'm witnessing, you know. That's the big thing." You may be turning him on to the Lord, but you can be sure that you're turning your boss off!

Your boss is thinking, "If that's Christianity, I want nothing to do with it." Be totally diligent in all that you do, as unto the Lord. People are watching and judging Christianity by the way I act and react. I should be as interested in the salvation of my boss and foreman as I am of the man working next to me. You can reach him at lunch time and after work. When you're employed, be honest in your labor and give an honest day's work for what you're being paid. Don't cheat by sloughing on your job.

If you love those that love you, that's *phileo*. Anybody can do that. Loving those that hate you, doing good to those that spitefully use you, that's *agape*. God has given you more than the natural human love. God has given you His kind of love that keeps on loving and doesn't ask for anything in return. Let God's love begin to flow through your life. The world today needs real examples of self-sacrificing love, willing to give without asking for a return.

What kind of spirit do you possess? A spirit of heaviness, fear, suspicion or murmuring, grumbling and complaining? Be thou an example of the spirit of Joy! That's what the Christian has—love, a spirit of confidence, and trust. It's sad that some Christians have a spirit of heaviness about them. They're either complaining and murmuring like the children of Israel, despairing, or walking around with a defeated attitude. Then they say: "Oh, you need to accept Jesus, brother. You need to get what I've got." Man, you've got the plague!

The world isn't looking for sorrow. They have enough sorrow. They have enough trouble. The world is looking for answers. They're looking for joy, peace, and confidence. As a believer in Jesus Christ and trusting in my Lord, I have great confidence that the Lord will work out every situation. I have great joy. I'm a child of God. I have great peace. Be thou an example of the believer, for people are watching what kind of spirit you possess.

How much real faith do you possess? How long must the headache persist till you quit praying about it and reach for the aspirin bottle? How long does it take to wear out your faith? How much does it take to destroy your confidence in God? How much does it take until you're convinced that God has forgotten you and doesn't care anymore, and you go back into the slough of despondency and despair?

"...Tried to start the car this morning. The battery's dead. I don't think God loves me anymore! God doesn't care about me. I'm not going to serve Him anymore." It's amazing how little it takes to knock the pins out from under a person!

Alexander the Great, an ardent admirer of Diogenes, had read his philosophies and was captivated by them. Diogenes was content to sit on a wash pail. That's all he possessed, but he was happy. Alexander possessed the world, but he was miserable.

One day Alexander the Great finally met Diogenes in person. Alexander was so excited that he said, "Diogenes, you're my master. I'm your disciple. I'll follow you all my life!" Diogenes took two fish, handed them to Alexander and said, "Carry these around in your pocket for two weeks." Alexander was incensed over the idea. "What do you mean! Smell like a fish for two weeks? Never!" Diogenes shook his head and said, "What a shame. Such devotion destroyed by two smelly fish."

Sometimes we say: "O God, I'll love You forever! I'll serve Thee, Lord. Wherever, whatever, anything! Lord, I'm Your disciple. I'll follow Thee!" The Lord gives us some little task, and we say, "Oh no, Lord. I'll never do that." The Lord shakes His head and says: "What a shame. Such devotion destroyed over a dead battery."

Have confidence in God. Know that God is going to work it out. Even though it's so black that there's no way out as far as you can see, absolutely hopeless as far as you can determine, have faith in God.

We're living in a polluted world. We're all aware of it and we hate it. Pollution is detestable. No one likes to look up into smog-filled skies. No one likes to see a polluted, clogged stream. We love pure air and pure water. But so many times we love a polluted mind. I'm convinced that man can survive the polluted air and the polluted water. It's the polluted mind that will destroy mankind.

You're living in a world in which the majority of the minds of men are polluted. You're living in a world today, in a society, in which anything goes. We've been taught that the mores determine what is right and what is wrong, because there's no absolute determination, no universal law of truth. Everything is relative to the society and to the mores. If the majority of the people are doing something, then it's no longer wrong—now it's right. You're being pressured because the mores of our society are polluted. Yet you're to be an example of the believer in purity.

I don't care whether the rest of the university is cohabiting together in their co-ed dorms, experimenting with premarital sex, or whatever—be thou an example of the believer in purity. That's what God desires of you. The Bible says, "Keep thyself pure" (1 Timothy 5:22). Keep your life pure, keep your body pure, keep your mind pure—for God! It doesn't matter whether the rest of the class has fallen into the quicksand of immoral rot and decay. "But the pressure is so heavy! The flesh is so weak. The opportunities are great and the temptations are multitude. I don't know if I can keep myself pure." The answer is that you probably can't. But I know One who can keep you.

The secret of being an example is to pay attention to and be diligent in the reading of the Word. Through the reading of the Scriptures you become strong, and not by any other way. One of our problems in Christianity today is looking for strength in areas outside the Word of God. You can never be strong apart from the Word of God. Experiences cannot make you strong in the Lord. Experiences don't help your spiritual maturity and growth.

We often have such confusion because of our spiritual experiences. We see people who have fantastic experiences. They have tremendous power. It seems they lay hands on the sick and the sick are healed. They're constantly telling us of their experiences of discernment or God speaking to them or seeing healings. They are all experience-oriented. Then we watch these people who have had such fantastic experiences, and then fall at a trial. Now our faith is shaken. We say, "Oh! I don't know.... They were so strong." They weren't necessarily strong. Experience is no criterion for spiritual strength. You don't grow strong by experiences. You're made strong through the Word of God. "I have written unto you, young men, because ye are strong, and the Word of God abideth in you" (1 John 2:14).

Your life is strengthened through the Word of God. You won't find strength apart from the Word of God, for it is the food that feeds the spiritual man. Spiritual anemia or weakness can always be traced back to the lack of knowledge and study of God's Word. Too many people are trying to grow on experience. You can't grow on experience. You can only grow on the Word of God. It provides the solid, substantial growth that you need. Get your foundation. "How firm a foundation, ye saints of the Lord, is laid for your faith in His excellent Word." Get rooted and grounded in the Word of God. Become strong in the Word of God!

These are the benefits you will gain from the Scriptures: *exhortation* and *doctrine*. This is what the Word of God actually is.

What is doctrine? Doctrine is correct belief. It will tell you what is the true and correct way. And Scripture does more—it encourages you to walk in the truth and in the way. Within the Scriptures is the encouragement to go ahead and do the right thing.

Each of us has been given a special talent, ability or ministry. When you first came to the Lord—that first, fresh blossom of God's love in your life—you used to go around singing all the time. You used to make up songs of love to the Lord. It was so glorious! It even seemed that God gave you a gift of singing and praising the Lord in song. What's happened? Why aren't you singing anymore?

"Well, they've never asked me to sing at Sunday morning service." But are you singing unto the Lord or unto man? You should sing to the Lord. It doesn't make any difference if man is listening or not. I'm not singing unto man, I'm singing unto the Lord. The beautiful thing is that the Lord appreciates it. Sometimes I sing for man; he doesn't appreciate it. But when I sing to the Lord, oh, it's so beautiful! I love singing to the Lord. Isn't that what the Scripture says? Sing unto the Lord a new song (Psalm 33:3). "Psalms and hymns and spiritual songs, singing and making melody in your heart to the Lord" (Ephesians 5:19).

When you're singing unto the Lord before man, man will be blessed by it, too. When you're singing unto man just to entertain, that's a sad trip. "I want men to know how well

I can sing. What fancy trills I can put into this number. I want them to know what a great musician I am." Then that's just what they'll get. They'll get the impression of your great musical abilities, but they won't be drawn to worship the Lord at all. Sing unto the Lord and men can identify with it and worship the Lord with you. Then you'll have a true ministry.

"Whatsoever ye do, do all to the glory of God" (1 Corinthians 10:31). Don't neglect that gift that is in you. Don't neglect that work that God began in your life. Timothy was evidently neglecting it. In the next epistle Paul said, "Stir up the gift of God, which is in thee" (2 Timothy 1:6). Stir it up! Sometimes we grow a little cold or stale. Start stirring up those things again—those expressions of love and praise unto our Lord.

Through our magazines, newspapers, television, and other media, it has become possible to know a little bit about everything. All of us have become somewhat versed in everything. We know a little bit about nuclear science, medicine, politics, diet—a little bit about everything. In reality, we don't know much about anything. We have become very broad but not very deep. Depth is something that is developed through meditation, and meditation is almost a lost art. How little we really meditate.

One morning the Lord set an alarm clock outside my window that went off before the alarm clock on the dresser. A mockingbird was singing glorious praises unto the Lord. I said, "Oh, mockingbird...praise the Lord! Just sing your praises to Him. Awake your morning, mockingbird, and praise God!" Because I had extra time that morning, I could spend some of it in meditation. With the accompaniment of the most beautiful music in the world, I began to think of the greatness, the love, and the goodness of God to me. As I began to think about my life, God's Spirit began to talk to me concerning my life as an example, and those areas where I'm failing and falling short. As the Spirit would bring them up I'd say, "Lord, strengthen me and help me in that area to be an example for Thee."

As you meditate on God's Word, God's truth, the greatness of God, and the work of God's Spirit within your life, God begins to work within you. You're then enabled to be the example of the believer that He would have you to be. You're to be an example through meditation on His Word—wholly giving yourself over to purity, faith, righteous conduct, clean speech, and the love of God working in you.

Paul describes the results of being an example of the believer: in saving others you will also be saving yourself. This is the truth of God. Mark it carefully.

You cannot minister to other people without God ministering to you also. You cannot give without God giving to you. "With what measure ye [give], it shall be measured to you again" (Matthew 7:2). You cannot help others without God helping you. You cannot seek the blessing of others without God blessing you. So many times while praying for God to heal someone else, God healed me; or to strengthen someone else, God strengthened me; or to comfort someone else, God comforted me. When I'm giving out, I find that God is giving back to me. That is a glorious fact of God!

If you sow sparingly, you'll reap sparingly. If you sow bountifully, you'll reap bountifully. You're going to reap what you sow (Galatians 6:7). That is God's law of nature. You want a huge harvest? Plant a huge crop of seeds. You want a few ears of corn? Drop a few grains of corn into the dirt. It's a law of life. We're so interested in God ministering to us that we get self-oriented. "What's God going to do for me? If I minister to them, I won't have time to take care of my own needs."

One time, there was a man who was lost in a snowstorm. He could only see a few feet in front of him. This man had trudged for hours in the blizzard. Finally, he stumbled and fell down in the snow. He thought, "I'm too tired! I can't lift myself up. I'll just sleep for a few moments. Maybe then I can get going again." And that deadly lethargy started to take hold of him.

But, suddenly, he discovered that the object over which he had stumbled was a body. He began to brush away the snow and found that there was a pulse in the body—he was still alive! "Oh, I've got to help him. I've got to save him!" In a super-human effort the man stood to his feet, put the body over his shoulders, and started to trudge through the blizzard once more. It was just a few yards away that he came to a cabin. He found that he was saved by saving another. This is so often true. In saving others we ourselves are saved, in ministering to others we ourselves receive.

As you're an example of the believers and as you give heed to these things, you'll find that God, in turn, will minister back to you all that is necessary to be what He has called you to be.

If all the Christians were just like you—if they served the Lord as diligently as you serve the Lord, if they loved the Lord as deeply as you love the Lord, if they were as faithful to God as you are faithful to God, if they would follow your example—what kind of church would exist today?

How many prayer meetings would be canceled for lack of attendance? How many Bible studies would be set aside? How many missionaries would be called home for lack of support? What kind of church would it be if you set the example for all the believers of how they should love, how they should serve, how they should give?

# CHAPTER 11

# QUESTIONS & ANSWERS

We're very happy to answer your questions as best as we're able. Some of the issues I don't understand and don't have an answer for—but, as much as possible, we're taking your Bible questions and giving you biblical answers.

**Q: What do you think of Christians going dancing, listening to rock 'n' roll music, going to the movies, or watching TV?**

**A:** This is a problem of Christian liberty—just what I can and cannot do as a child of God.

First of all, I don't feel that we can set rules for Christian activities. I believe this is definitely a matter of one's own individual conscience. The Bible says, "Who art thou that judgest another man's servant? To his own master he standeth or falleth;... For God is able to make him to stand" (Romans 14:4).

As a Christian I'm probably one of the most liberated persons in the world! We hear a lot today about human rights, freedom, liberty. But those who aren't Christians really don't know anything at all about liberty, because they're bound by the power of Satan and darkness. They have no true liberty.

As Christians it's glorious to have the freedom we have in Christ Jesus. People look upon Christianity as very restrictive because churches have made a lot of rules. They have tried to tell you what you can and can't do as a Christian. However, the Bible doesn't make any such listings for us.

Certain Scriptures give us guidelines. In John we read, "Love not the world, neither the things that are in the world. If any man love the world, the love of the Father is not in him" (1 John 2:15). Paul the apostle declares, "All things are lawful for me..." (1 Corinthians 6:12). I don't know of any broader theological or philosophical ethic than that! Paul also declares, "There is therefore now no condemnation to them which are in Christ Jesus" (Romans 8:1).

Paul the apostle says, "All things are lawful for me." I think that this goes into the area of entertainment, dancing, or the kind of music I listen to. But just a minute! Paul didn't stop there. Though I have a total freedom and there is no condemnation, Paul said, "...all things are not expedient." Expedient means "to help along the way." The idea is that, as a Christian, I'm running in a race. Paul said, "Know ye not that they which run in a race run all, but one receiveth the prize?" (1 Corinthians 9:24). There are things that can impede my progress, which can slow me down. They can keep me from winning the race. We are told to lay aside every weight and sin which so easily besets us, that we might run with patience the race that is set before us (Hebrews 12:1–2). These activities can become weights.

My goal is to be found in Christ Jesus, not having my own righteousness, but the righteousness which is of Christ through faith. I don't want a legal righteousness based upon my obedience to man-made rules. My righteousness isn't established by my activities; it is through my faith in Jesus Christ! It's totally incorrect to say, "Since I don't go to the movies or clubs, this makes me more righteous." It's not a matter of righteousness, it's just a matter of expedience.

I don't want to depend on any kind of righteousness that I could achieve by my own actions, activities, works, or goodness. The only righteousness with which I can stand before God is that righteousness imparted to me by faith in Jesus Christ.

There are things that impede my walk. Thus, though it might be lawful for me, that is, it wouldn't send me to hell, yet because it would impede my walk, I won't do it. Paul went on to say, "All things are lawful for me,...but all things edify not" (1 Corinthians 10:23). There are some things that have a tendency to tear me down and draw me away from Christ, rather than to build me up in Jesus Christ. My desire is to be built up in Christ and to draw close to Him.

Though an activity may be lawful for me and I can prove that it's not wrong, yet by the same token, it doesn't build me up in Christ. If it takes me away from Jesus, then I want nothing to do with it.

Finally Paul said, "All things are lawful for me, but I will not be brought under the power of any." I have glorious liberty in Christ. I have been set free from the power of my flesh, which ruled over me for so long. If I go right back into something that brings me under its power, then I'm no longer free.

So, enjoying my freedom as I do, I won't exercise my freedom in such a way as to bring myself into bondage. However, if I exercise my freedom in that way, I'm actually destroying the very freedom I enjoy because now my mind is under the control or influence of, say, alcohol. In exercising my freedom to drink I may become an alcoholic, and I'm no longer free. If my mind comes under the control of the alcohol so that I don't respond or react as I normally would, then I'm no longer free. I love my freedom so much that I won't allow my mind to be brought under the power of any influence other than God's glorious Holy Spirit. I don't think that, as Christians, we can draw the fine line between what is right and what is wrong. The whole issue is, "What is pleasing to the Father?" I want to do all things that are pleasing to Him. So, I measure my activities by how they affect my relationship to God, my Christian walk, and finally, my Christian witness.

**Q: Is it wrong for women to wear pantsuits?**

**A:** Let me say, I think it's wrong for some women I have seen to wear pantsuits! However, I don't know of any Scripture that would prohibit women from wearing pantsuits. There is a Scripture that speaks against women wearing men's apparel (Deuteronomy 22:5). But I surely wouldn't wear one of those pantsuits and, thus I don't call it men's apparel. I think they're designed for women. In some cases and in some activities, a pantsuit can be much more modest than a dress. I really have no problem with women wearing pantsuits. I don't think you can make a scriptural case against women wearing pantsuits.

**Q: I have a friend who is a Seventh-day Adventist. He says that God will reject me for not going to church on Saturday. What does the Bible say?**

**A:** I'm glad the Bible doesn't say what your friend says. In Romans 14:5, Paul said that one man esteems one day above another while another man esteems every day alike. "Let every man be fully persuaded in his own mind."

Your friend esteems one day above another, and he esteems Saturday to be the day to worship the Lord as the holy day. As far as my own personal feelings are concerned, I esteem every day alike, because every day to me is a holy day to worship the Lord. It is something I don't have any problem with, because I just love the Lord and worship Him continually.

When the Sabbath day law was given in the Book of Exodus, God declared that it was to be a perpetual covenant between Him and the nation Israel. "It is a sign between me and the children of Israel for ever" (Exodus 31:17). Nothing is ever said concerning observance of the Sabbath day by Gentiles.

As recorded in Acts, the early church elders met together to write to the Gentiles in regards to keeping the Law. Peter asked, "Why should we put on them a yoke that neither we nor our fathers were able to bear?" (Acts 15:10). There were certain "Judaizers" from the church in Jerusalem who went to the Gentile fellowship in Antioch. They told those at Antioch that unless they kept the Law of Moses and were circumcised, they couldn't be saved.

The Seventh-day Adventists are much like these Judaizers who were creating problems in the church in Antioch. But the elders in Jerusalem only told the Gentile believers that they shouldn't eat anything strangled and to keep themselves from fornication. If they would do this, they did well. The elders didn't try to place the Gentile believers under the Sabbath day law at all!

Paul tells us in Colossians 2 that Christ blotted out the handwriting of ordinances that were against us. This, of course, is in reference to the Sabbath day law and all the other such ordinances. Jesus took them out of the way. He nailed them to His cross. He made an open display of His victory over them, triumphing over them in the cross. Because of this, Paul said, "Let no man therefore judge you in meat, or in drink, or in respect of a holyday, or of the new moon, or of the Sabbath days: which are a shadow of things to come" (Colossians 2:16, 17).

These things were all just shadows in the Old Testament of that which was to come, which was Jesus Christ. The Sabbath day was a shadow of the rest we as the children of God would experience in Christ. We have the substance, Jesus Christ. Therefore, the shadows that spoke of the substance have no hold on us. I'm not required to keep the Sabbath day law any longer.

If I seek righteousness by the keeping of the Sabbath day, then it would be important that I keep the Sabbath day completely. The law declares that I'm not to kindle any fire on the Sabbath. Therefore, I should turn down the thermostat in the house, because, if I allow the furnace to go on, I'm kindling a fire. I shouldn't start my car, because I'm kindling a fire in the combustion chambers the moment I turn on the engine. Thus, I couldn't drive anywhere. I would have to limit my walking to two-thirds of a mile. I would have to keep all of these little regulations!

In the Talmud, the Jews sought to determine what constituted bearing a burden on the Sabbath day. According to their final interpretation, if you wore false teeth you were bearing a burden. So, you couldn't wear your false teeth on the Sabbath!

I'm glad that I have this glorious liberty in Christ, and I don't have to worry about those kinds of things. Jesus Christ has set me free from these ordinances of the law. My righteousness is now through faith in Him. Because of my faith in Christ, God will accept me, even as He accepted Abraham long before the law was ever given. Abraham believed God, and it was his faith that was imputed to him for righteousness. God accepts me on the basis of my faith, not on the basis of the day that I worship Him. Thank God for that!

**Q: Would you have any suggestions for someone with a non-degree business background who sincerely desires to teach God's Word?**

**A:** Yes, I surely would. Study the Word of God! Really get into it. Then, open up your home and start a home Bible study. Take a particular book, say the Book of Philippians. If you want to write to The Word For Today, we'll be glad to give you a list of some excellent commentaries on the various books of the Bible. You could also get our commentary tapes on the book you choose to teach. Then, just start teaching!

The best way to learn is to teach. Paul the apostle may have had some degree in the Hebrew school, but he certainly never attended seminary. Peter, James, John, and the rest of the disciples never attended a formal college. Yet, they all became teachers. God's ordination is never of man. That which qualifies you is the desire God has placed upon your heart. If you really have the desire to teach, go for it!

The main point is to prepare yourself. God uses prepared vessels. So, prepare yourself in the Word. It may be that you need to prepare yourself in a school. Some people do, because they don't have enough gumption to be

self-starters. Others are self-starters. I don't know whether
a school is going to do that much for you. Paul the apostle
went out to the desert after his conversion and for three
years was taught by the Holy Spirit in Arabia. I know of
no better schooling than just waiting upon the Lord, getting
some good commentaries, and studying. Certainly, God
can use you!

**Q: Is a person who commits suicide totally lost for
eternity?**

**A:** Definitely not! I believe that a person who is driven
to the point of committing suicide no longer has full
responsibility for the things he's doing. Driven to a point of
such mental extremes, he isn't necessarily responsible for
the action of taking his own life. Certainly, Scripture
doesn't indicate anywhere that this is an unpardonable
sin. The only sin for which there is no forgiveness is that of
rejecting Jesus Christ as your Lord and Savior.

**Q: You mentioned that the Antichrist will be blind in
one eye and paralyzed in one arm. Where does the
Bible say that?**

**A:** In the Book of Zechariah the prophet is dealing with
the true shepherd and with the false shepherd. Jesus
Christ, of course, is the true shepherd who was coming.
Then Zechariah talks about the false shepherd that would
arise.

In Zechariah 11:15–17 he wrote, "And the Lord said
unto me, Take unto thee yet the instruments of a foolish
shepherd. For, lo, I will raise up a shepherd in the land,
which shall not visit those that be cut off, neither shall seek
the young one, nor heal that that is broken, nor feed that
that standeth still: but he shall eat the flesh of the fat, and
tear their claws in pieces. Woe to the idle shepherd that

leaveth his flock! The sword shall be upon his arm, and upon his right eye: his arm shall be [shriveled] up, and his right eye shall be utterly darkened." This is a prophecy referring to the Antichrist about his right arm being paralyzed and his right eye blinded. Revelation 13:3 also speaks of his miraculous healing from a deadly wound on his head.

**Q: John 1:12 says, "To them gave He power to become the sons of God, even to them that believe on his name." Does this refer to those who believe in Jesus but haven't received the fullness of the Spirit? If so, will they have a different position in the coming Kingdom?**

A: The first chapter of John introduces Jesus Christ, declaring that He is God come in the flesh. "The Word was made flesh, and dwelt among us... He came to His own, and His own received Him not." "His own" refers to the Jewish people. Jesus came to the Jews, but they rejected Him as their Messiah.

So, as many as received Him, to them gave He the power to become the sons of God, even to those that believe in His name. This is a reference to anyone, Jew or Gentile, who believes in Jesus Christ. Such a person has been given the "power" (the word here means "authority") to become the son of God. The question of having received the fullness of the Spirit doesn't have anything to do with our relationship to God in heaven. I believe that if we have received Jesus Christ as our Savior, we have received the Spirit. It's up to us to yield ourselves fully to the work of the Holy Spirit in our lives. Every born-again child of God has the Holy Spirit in his life. God desires that our cup overflows, that we might experience the beautiful overflowing of the Holy Spirit.

As for our place in the coming Kingdom, I feel that there will definitely be degrees of position and rewards in heaven. This is certainly brought out by Jesus Christ. We should be concerned with our rewards in heaven (Matthew 6:19–20). In reality, these will be predicated upon our faithful stewardship with the things that God has entrusted to us in this life. Have I been a faithful steward of those things that God has placed in my hands?

Certainly, the fullness of the Spirit in my life helps me to be a faithful witness for God. I need the power and the fullness of the Spirit, but it's just to help me and assist me in my walk here on Earth. It really has nothing to do, as far as I understand, with our rewards in heaven.

Q: When an animal dies, does its soul simply go out of existence?

A: The Bible doesn't tell us anything about the future of an animal's soul. Since the soul is the consciousness, it definitely appears that the consciousness of an animal ceases to exist when it dies. So, I'm of the opinion that its life completely ceases at death. However, the Scripture is totally silent on this particular subject. Thus, there's no way to answer the question, except in the form of conjecture and opinion.

Let me tell you one thing. My opinion isn't worth very much at all on any subject. It is what God has to say that's important. There are certain questions that, if I cannot answer from the Scriptures, I'd rather not give an answer at all. It's only then my opinion on a subject, and that's of practically no value.

Q: Is there anything in the Bible that explains the possible existence of unidentified flying objects? Could

**alien beings have anything to do with the end times prophecies?**

A: Many people who believe in flying saucers often point to the vision in Ezekiel chapter 1. The prophet saw the wheel within the wheel, heard the noise of the wheels, etc. Was Ezekiel sighting a flying saucer?

It's important to note that when Ezekiel described his vision, he was actually describing cherubim (Ezekiel 10), angelic beings that worship around the throne of God. These cherubim are a class of angelic beings. The prophet was describing what cherubim looked like, how they moved, and their sounds.

At the time Satan rebelled against God, he himself was one of the cherubim. We are told that he was the anointed cherub that covereth (Ezekiel 28:14). He had been in Eden, the Garden of God. When he fell, Satan took a third part of the angelic beings with him (Revelation 12:4, 9). These fallen angels allied themselves with Satan in his rebellion against God.

So, since Satan was a cherub, perhaps other cherubim went with him in his revolt. It's quite possible that the sighting of these supposed flying saucers, with their movements and lights, are actually evil spirits, cherubim or other spirit beings controlled by Satan. Thus, UFO's could come from the realm of the spirit world, and people may actually be seeing the spirit world of fallen angels, who have the appearance of a wheel within a wheel, making whirring sounds, etc.

Outside of this reference, I don't know of any Scripture that would confirm the fact that alien beings have anything to do with the end-times prophecies. However, with the increasing reports of UFO activity, it may be one of the explanations offered to those who remain on the earth after the rapture, the sudden disappearance of millions of people.

**Q: In John 15:6 it appears that anyone who doesn't produce fruit will be cast "into the fire." But 1 Corinthians 3:15 says that a person whose works are burned up will be saved "as by fire." I'm confused. Is there any difference between the fruit and the works? How does this relate to salvation?**

**A:** In John's Gospel, Jesus was talking about the necessity of abiding in Him. If you don't abide in Him, you cannot be saved, and you cannot bear fruit. Such people who don't bear fruit will be gathered and burned, because they're not saved. The passage in 1 Corinthians talks about the works I do as a child of God with the wrong motivation. I may be motivated with the desire to glorify myself or receive praise from men. Such works performed by a Christian will be burned up, though he will be saved, even as by fire.

**Q: I want so much to open my heart to Jesus, to walk with Him and live by His Word, but I've been sinning all my life. Even though I love God, I still sin a lot. Does God still love me? Does He forgive people who aren't good Christians? How can I feel He's always with me and still loves me when I sin so much?**

**A:** You can only feel it as you believe His promise to you: God's love is unconditional. God doesn't love good children and hate bad children. God loves good and bad children alike! You need to realize that glorious grace God has extended toward you and receive His love and grace— even though you realize more and more how totally undeserving you are of that love. I have discovered that accepting grace gracefully is difficult, but I'm slowly learning how to do it.

"If we say that we have no sin, we deceive ourselves, and the truth is not in us. If we confess our sins, he is faithful and just to forgive us our sins, and to cleanse us from all unrighteousness" (1 John 1:8–9). What is the sin for which a man will be condemned? It's the rejection of Jesus Christ. I have accepted Him. I still may be weak and fail, but at the base of my life is a love and a desire for Jesus Christ. That's what He counts for my righteousness— my faith in Him!

**Q: Is there any doctrine or scriptural proof that would support being slain in the Spirit?**

**A:** Using the Bible as our final authority for all faith and practice, we would have to confess that the Bible lacks any solid, scriptural evidence for this experience of being slain in the Spirit. Those who advocate this experience seek to point out that Daniel fell on his face before the Lord when the angel of the Lord appeared to him.

In the Garden of Gethsemane Jesus asked the soldiers, "Whom seek ye?" They said, "Jesus of Nazareth." He said, "I am He," after which the soldiers fell over backward. Some people refer to that as being slain in the Spirit. Then, they refer to Paul the apostle on the road to Damascus. But none of these cases are anything like the experience that people today refer to as being slain in the Spirit.

We don't read of Jesus laying hands on people and of them being slain in the Spirit. Nor do we find any teaching on it in the Book of Acts or in the epistles. Thus, I reject it as an unscriptural experience.

Is it of God? I don't know. There is one Scripture I find on the subject. It is in the Old Testament (2 Kings 19:35). One night the angel of the Lord went through the camp of the Assyrians. In the morning, the Assyrians were all laying around dead. The angel of the Lord had smitten them that night. The Scripture says, "And the slain of the Lord were many." They were literally slain by the Spirit!

It is an experience, and there are those who would seek to create a doctrine on the basis of the experience. I run from such things. I really want no part of something for which I cannot give solid scriptural evidence.

# CHAPTER 12

# UNTO US A SON IS GIVEN

> For unto us a child is born, unto us a son is given: and the government shall be upon his shoulder: and his name shall be called Wonderful, Counselor, The mighty God, The everlasting Father, The Prince of Peace. Of the increase of his government and peace there shall be no end, upon the throne of David, and upon his kingdom, to order it, and to establish it with judgment and with justice from henceforth even for ever. The zeal of the LORD of hosts will perform this (Isaiah 9:6–7).

Isaiah is looking at two aspects of the birth of Christ. First of all, he sees the human side. Isaiah declared, "For unto us a child is born." It must be recognized that the child who was born, and about whom Isaiah prophesied, was unlike any other child ever born. For this child had no human father. Isaiah had predicted this in the seventh chapter. "Behold, a virgin shall conceive, and bear a son, and shall call his name Immanuel" (Isaiah 7:14). The name Immanuel means "God with us."

The child who was born was the fulfillment of God's promise to man in the Garden of Eden. God had said that the woman's seed—intimating the virgin birth—would bruise the head, or authority, of the serpent (Genesis 3:15). This child was to destroy the power and authority of Satan in our lives and to bring us victory over the power of darkness.

This child who was born was unlike any child ever born. So many facets of His life were predicted in the Scriptures. Where He was to be born, the circumstances around His birth, the events in His early childhood and in His ministry, etc. These events were predicted in more than 300 prophecies of the Old Testament. This child who was born was heralded by the angels. At the time of His birth there were in the same country shepherds keeping watch over their flocks at night. And the angel of the Lord appeared to them, and the glory of the Lord shone round about them. The shepherds were frightened. But the angel said,

> Fear not: for, behold, I bring you good tidings of great joy, which shall be to all people. For unto you is born this day in the city of David a Saviour, which is Christ the Lord. Suddenly, there was with the angel a multitude of the heavenly host, praising God and saying, Glory to God in the highest, and on earth peace, good will toward men (Luke 2:10–11, 13–14).

This child who was born was destined for greatness. For we read in Isaiah's prophecy, "And the government shall be upon his shoulder: and his name shall be called Wonderful, Counselor, The mighty God, The everlasting Father, The Prince of Peace. Of the increase of his government and peace there shall be no end, upon the throne of David and his kingdom, to order it, and to establish it with judgment and with justice from henceforth even for ever." The power of God was to rest upon this child. He was to rule over the world as King of Kings and Lord of Lords.

But this child who was born was also destined for suffering. Isaiah wrote, "He is despised and rejected of men; a man of sorrows, and aquainted with grief:...he was despised, and we esteemed him not" (Isaiah 53:3).

His suffering was also spoken of by Simeon the priest, the aged man who had a glorious secret of God within his heart. God had spoken to him and said, "You will not die until you see the Messiah." As Mary and Joseph brought this child to the temple to offer sacrifices for the first-born, to redeem him and to present him to the Lord, Simeon was brought to them by the Spirit. He took the child into his arms and lifted him up to heaven. He cried, "Lord, now lettest thou thy servant depart in peace,...for mine eyes have seen thy salvation" (Luke 2:29).

Then Simeon prophesied concerning the child. "This child is set for the fall and rising again of many in Israel. And he shall be a light to the Gentiles." And then speaking directly to Mary, Simeon said, "And a sword shall also pierce through your own soul"—referring to the pain Mary would experience when she saw her child hanging on a cross, mocked, despised, and rejected by men.

The child was born to die upon a cross. When Pilate talked to Him, Jesus said, "To this end was I born, that I might be the King." Daniel prophesied that He would be cut off without receiving the kingdom (Daniel 9:26).

How can we reconcile a child destined for greatness and also destined for suffering? Destined to reign forever, yet destined to be cut off without receiving the kingdom? It is reconciled in the fact that this child who was born in

Bethlehem is coming back again to reign as King of Kings and Lord of Lords!

Jesus said, "Then shall appear the sign of the Son of man in heaven:...and they shall see the Son of man coming in the clouds of heaven with power and great glory" (Matthew 24:30). As Jesus left Earth from the Mount of Olives, the disciples saw the clouds receive Him until He went out of their sight. The men in white apparel said, "Men of Galilee, why stand ye gazing up into heaven? this same Jesus, which is taken up from you into heaven, shall so come in like manner" (Acts 1:11). He is coming again as King of Kings and Lord of Lords to establish it in judgment and justice from henceforth even forever. That portion of Isaiah's prophecy shall be fulfilled at the Second Coming of Jesus Christ.

Unto us a child is born—destined to suffer, and yet destined to reign forever. That's looking at the birth of Jesus from the human side.

Looking at the birth of Jesus from the divine side, the prophet declared, "Unto us a son is given." This child who was born was, in reality, a Son who was given. For God so loved the world that He gave His only begotten Son (John 3:16).

---

*God gave His Son, so that the Son might reveal to us the truth about the Father.*

---

Man's concepts of God had become so totally garbled and confused that man no longer knew the truth about God. Just read the ideas about God in the Greek and

Roman mythologies. You'll see how man lost all sense of truth about God. Even the nation Israel, the people God had revealed Himself to in the clearest fashion, was confused about God. The teachers, scribes, and Pharisees, who pretended to know more about God than anybody else, were constantly rebuked by Jesus, because they taught the wrong things about God. They gave the people a totally wrong concept of God. "Woe unto you, scribes and Pharisees, hypocrites!" (Luke 11:44). They completely misrepresented God to the people, and so the people didn't know or understand Him.

A Son was given to us to reveal the Father, so that we might know the Father *in truth*. The people had been taught to think of God as some cruel and vengeful judge, ready and anxious to destroy them. In reality, He was a heartbroken Father, grieving because His children were lost.

---

*The essential truth that Jesus taught about God was that God has an undying love for you.*

---

God wants to display and demonstrate all of His love to you in the fullest and richest way. "God is love" (1 John 4:8).

### The Purpose of the Son

A Son is given so that He might teach us the truth about God and His love for us. A Son is given so that we might again have fellowship with God, that we might come back to God's first and original intent for man.

When God created man, His purpose was that man might enjoy constant and beautiful fellowship with Him. So, God placed man in the Garden of Eden. The Bible speaks about God coming into the Garden and walking with man, communing and talking with him. God's intent for man was fulfilled as Adam walked in fellowship with God.

But we read that Adam disobeyed and that sin entered the world. Adam's fellowship with God was broken as the result of sin. This is always the effect of sin. For Isaiah tells us that God's hand is not short that He cannot save, neither is His ear heavy that He cannot hear. But your sins have separated you from your God (Isaiah 59:1–2). Sin always separates a man from God.

A Son is given to bring us back into fellowship with God. In order to do that, He must take care of the sin problem. We read that God made Him who knew no sin to be sin for us, that we might be made the righteousness of God through Him (2 Corinthians 5:21). "All we like sheep have gone astray; we have turned every one to his own way; and the LORD hath laid on him the iniquity of us all" (Isaiah 53:6).

Jesus came to us. He was given by God to remove from us the sin which had destroyed our fellowship with God, and to restore us to fellowship with God.

John wrote, "That which was from the beginning, which we have heard, which we have seen with our eyes, which we have looked upon, and our hands have handled, of the Word of life; (for the life was manifested, and we have seen it, and bear witness, and show unto you that eternal life, which was with the Father, and was manifested unto us;) that which we have seen and heard declare we unto you, that ye also may have fellowship with us: and truly our fellowship is with the Father, and with his Son Jesus Christ. And these things write we unto you, that your joy may be full" (1 John 1:1–4).

If you say that you have fellowship with God and you're walking in darkness, you're lying. You don't know the truth. But if you walk in the light as He is in the light, then you have fellowship with God—and the blood of Jesus Christ, God's Son, is continually cleansing you from all sin. Unto us a Son is given to bring us into fellowship with God by continually cleansing us from all sin, thus keeping us in continual fellowship with God.

A Son is given that He might be the Savior of the world. The whole world is lost in the darkness of sin, but the light of the world is Jesus. Paul said that the Gentiles were without God and without hope in the world. But unto us a Son is given who might lead us from that darkness into the light of God, that through Him we might experience the love of God. He is that true light that lights every man who comes into the world.

### The Reactions to the Son

What was the world's reaction to this child who was born, this Son who was given? Jesus always evoked sharp emotional responses from people. They either hated Him or loved Him. Some people said, "We will not have Him rule over us!" They hated the light that He brought, because the light revealed the truth about themselves. The light revealed the fraud and sham of their own existence. They wouldn't come to that light, and they nailed the Son to the cross. As he hung on the cross, they mocked, jeered, and taunted Him. He was despised and rejected.

There was another crowd at the cross. It was much smaller. These people were weeping and sobbing, because they loved the Son, and He was suffering. They had submitted their lives to Him, to serve Him and to live for Him with everything they had.

There is a sharp contrast between the two reactions to the child who was born and the Son who was given.

Though 2,000 years have now passed, and man has supposedly made great strides in his cultural and social development, we find that these same two emotional responses are still evoked by Jesus Christ. Today, people either love Him or hate Him. Some people still become violent in their reactions to Him. If they could they'd crucify Him again. They're still crying out, "We will not have Him to rule over us!" They would like to get rid of Christ and the influence of Christianity in the world today. For they love their darkness rather than the light, because their deeds are evil.

On the other hand, some have rejoiced in that light and have found glorious fellowship with God. They walk in the light, thanking God that they know and have fellowship with Him once again.

One of the saddest Scriptures in the Bible is found in the first chapter of John's Gospel. "In the beginning was the Word, and the Word was with God, and the Word was God. The same was in the beginning with God. All things were made by him; and without him was not any thing made that was made" (John 1:1-3). Look around. Everything you see was made by Him. "In him was life, and the life was the light of men...That was the true Light, which lighteth every man that cometh into the world" (vv. 4, 9). And this is the Scripture that has such pathos and sorrow: "He was in the world, and the world was made by him, and the world knew him not" (v. 10).

Jesus was walking around, looking at all the life forms that He had created. He understood completely the genetic codes within the cells long before men stumbled onto these truths. But men had become so alienated from God in their minds and consciousness that when God walked among them they didn't recognize Him. The world "knew him not. He came unto his own [the Jewish people], and his own received him not. But as many as received him, to them gave he power to become the sons of God, even to them that believe on his name" (John 1:10b–12).

Unto us a Son is given...to bring us into fellowship with God by taking away our sins and dying in our place. He thus became the light of the world and the hope of mankind.

Today, you are in one of two groups: those who have a right to celebrate Christmas, and those who through their celebration of Christmas are guilty of the greatest hypocrisy. If you have received the Christ of Christmas, then the joy and peace of fellowship with God is yours. For unto us a child is born, unto us a Son is given. Have you received this, the greatest gift of all?

# CHAPTER 13

# THE SIN OF SODOM

> Behold, this was the iniquity of thy sister
> Sodom, pride, fulness of bread, and abundance
> of idleness was in her and in her daughters,
> neither did she strengthen the hand of the poor
> and needy (Ezekiel 16:49).

Whenever we talk about the sin of Sodom we go back to
the Book of Genesis, when the Lord appeared unto
Abraham and told him that He, with the angels, was going
to the city of Sodom to bring the judgment of God. When
the angels arrived at the city of Sodom, they were met by
Lot, who was sitting at the gate; and Lot invited them to
his home for the evening (Genesis 18:1, 2, 16, 20–22; 19:1–
3).

But after supper the men of Sodom began to beat on the
door of Lot's house, demanding that Lot send out the two
young men in order that they might engage in homosexual
relations with them. Lot protested against this evil, and
the men then turned against Lot as a stranger among them
who was now seeking to be their judge. When they
threatened physical violence against Lot, the angels drew
Lot back into the house and shut the door, smiting the men

of Sodom with blindness so that they groped all night trying to find the door of Lot's house (Genesis 19:4–11).

The angels of the Lord then said unto Lot, "Get out of here! We're going to destroy this city. Flee with your family and all who will go with you. The judgment of God is going to fall against this wickedness!"

The angels of the Lord then led Lot forth from the city, and the fire of God's judgment came and destroyed the cities of Sodom and Gomorrah because of their exceeding wickedness and sinfulness before God. And so we have the term "sodomy," by which is expressed the obvious sin of Sodom. But as God looks back and analyzes the sin of Sodom, He sees it in its more subtle form, in its roots, before it bore fruit.

There are certain roots when tolerated that will germinate into vile fruit. Homosexuality and sodomy were actually the final manifestations of the people's sin. Their sin had been germinating under the soil for a long time before being manifested in its final form.

### Pride

In Ezekiel 16:49 as God declares "the iniquity of thy sister Sodom," God emphasized that the sin of Sodom was actually pride. Pride is thinking of yourself more highly than you should; it is an exalted opinion of yourself. So many times we look at the blessings that God has granted to us, and we act as though our genius, abilities, or wit have brought God's favor and blessings upon our lives not realizing that if we have anything worthwhile and good within us, it has come from God.

The Bible says, "For I say...to every man that is among you, not to think of himself more highly than he ought to think" (Romans 12:3). Again the Bible says, "Let each esteem others better than themselves" (Philippians 2:3). Esteeming yourself above others is pride, and it is a deadly sin.

When God speaks of the pride of Sodom, we must recognize that He's talking of a nationalistic pride, because Sodom was a city-state. But you say, "Just a minute, Chuck. Shouldn't we be proud that we are Americans?" I believe that we should take pride in our country, but the danger is that so often we do not give credit where credit is due. In looking at our nation and the greatness it has achieved, we need to recognize that our greatness came to us from God—that it was God who made our nation strong. Our early forefathers recognized this. Katharine Lee Bates wrote, "America, America, God shed His grace on thee," and that is the secret of the greatness of our nation. God's grace has been shed upon us.

And yet there are those today who say that our system has made us great. They would attribute the strength of our nation to free enterprise. Of course, free enterprise is almost becoming an historic term at this point, as we see more and more government regulations placed on the businesses. They are making it almost impossible to conduct business profitably or efficiently. It is as though they seek to make business as inept as government.

There are others who in looking at the nation take pride in our Constitution. They say it is because of our Constitution that we have such a strong and powerful nation. Certainly our Constitution was formed by prayer; men sought the guidance of God in the framing of the Constitution—but unfortunately today our Constitution is being perverted and misinterpreted by our courts.

Now according to the courts you can teach the Bible in school as a book of literature, as mythology, or the superstitious writings of ancient people—but you cannot teach it as the Word of God. You can use the name of Jesus Christ in your classroom as long as it is an oath or in blasphemy, but you cannot speak in terms of reverence or worship or as the Savior. You can talk about Jesus as the son of man, but you cannot speak of Him as the Son of God. You can post the Communist Manifesto on the walls of the classroom, but not the Ten Commandments.

"America, America, God shed His grace on thee." Unfortunately, through some of the rulings of the courts, the honoring of God and recognition of the secret of strength has been twisted and changed, so that rather than knowing the grace of God, America is being ripened for the judgment of God.

"America, America, God shed His grace on thee," but America, what are you doing? You're destroying the very foundations that have made you great, and you're ripening for the judgment of God.

Many people take pride in our military superiority. They believe that our military prowess has made our country strong and great. These people unfortunately are ignoring the facts of history, for every major empire that toppled, fell at the peak of its military might. Military strength alone was never an insurance to any nation or guarantee of safety.

Concerning the destruction that was to come against Israel, God said, "That he would bring the Assyrians against the hypocritical people" (Isaiah 10:5, 6). If there was ever a nation of hypocrisy, it is America, which once knew the grace of God. They write on their coins, "In God we trust," and now they use them for every devilish and damnable purpose.

As God saw it, the sin of Sodom was pride—the failure to recognize God as the source of strength, power, and might.

## Prosperity

The second sin of Sodom was the fullness of bread. They had become fat. They were a prosperous people and, becoming fat, they became weak.

One of the thrilling aspects of visiting Israel is to see a nation that is young, so filled with national spirit that when the people talk about their nation a quiver comes into their voices and an intensity in their spirit; for they realize that their survival depends upon God and being unified together under God—and that is their only hope of survival. To see the intensity of these people is a beautiful and rewarding experience.

But we have become independent of God. We feel that we can now rule Him out of our national life. We can set Him aside. After all, are we not strong? Have we not developed to such a high degree that we no longer need God?

Oh, our Founding Fathers were superstitious, and they thought it was necessary to establish a nation upon God and trust in God. Now we've become enlightened, and we realize that it wasn't necessary at all... and we are destroying the very pillars that have held up our nation.

## *Idleness*

Another sin that God saw in Sodom was their idleness, "and abundance of idleness." The abundance of idleness led to a misuse of Sodom's idle time.

When I was a small boy, my mother used to constantly tell me, "Charles, an idle mind is the Devil's workshop." Keep your mind active, study, keep learning. Don't let your mind be idle. It used to be that a 60-hour work week was very common. No one thought anything about it. But as the labor unions began to form and the movement began to grow, their cry was for a 48-hour work week. After that goal was achieved, they began to cry for a 40-hour work week. Now they are crying for a four-day work week. The purpose is to give men more time on the weekend for leisure and for their pursuit of pleasure.

You ask, "Chuck, are you opposed to labor?" No. I believe that the labor movement has brought a lot of good to our society. What I am opposed to is the way people spend their leisure time. We're living in a nation that has gone pleasure-mad. Everything is designed and geared to fill the abundance of idleness with pleasure. Men are using that idle time to indulge themselves, and they're forgetting God and leaving Him out of their lives. How glorious if we could have a four-day work week, so that we would have three days to devote to serving the Lord completely and fully!

But the way men are proposing to use their abundance of idleness has become a national disgrace. The mistake and folly is that they think that through pleasure they can find the answers for their thirsty souls. However, the desire for pleasure is like a monster—the more you feed it, the more it demands. Experiences that used to bring a thrill and pleasure to you no longer bring the same thrill and pleasure, so you start looking for new experiences.

## Uncaring

The final sin of Sodom was that they did not strengthen the hand of the poor and needy. They became callous, uncaring, and indifferent to the needs of people around them, because they were so absorbed in themselves. They were no longer concerned with the needs of others.

These roots of sin in Sodom led to open and aggressive homosexuality. When the angels of the Lord came to the city of Sodom, the men began to beat at the door of the house of Lot. They were demanding that these men be sent out to them. The homosexuals had become so strong and this society had become so morally weak that the homosexuals felt a bravado, a freedom to express and manifest openly their impure and perverted desires.

Whenever a society is so weak that those who are perverted in their nature feel a bravery to expose themselves publicly, to make public demands, and become aggressive, then you have a society that is ready for the judgment of God.

As I look at our society in the United States today, and I see on the magazine racks and in the papers the aggressiveness of this segment of our society—the blatant openness with which they parade their sin—I realize how far down the road we have gone, and how near we are to the end.

"America, America, God shed His grace on thee," but we have sinned against the grace of God. We see within America today those very things that finally provoked the judgment of God and His destruction of the city of Sodom.

The bad seeds have produced the rotten fruit, and it is all around us: open, aggressive homosexuals. No more a sense of shame, but a demand for recognition and acceptance of their godless lifestyle. The men of Sodom began to publicly flaunt their sin, and they gave God no choice but judgment.

We begin to understand what Peter meant when he said, "judgment must begin at the house of God" (1 Peter 4:17). When we read of churches ordaining homosexuals and lesbians, the time is come for judgment. It must begin at the house of God, but if it first begins with us, what shall the end be of them that obey not the Gospel of God? And if the righteous scarcely be saved, where shall the ungodly and the sinner appear?

When I read the story about Lot, the city of Sodom, and its judgment, I'm encouraged by this fact: before God destroyed Sodom He first "delivered just Lot...that righteous man" (2 Peter 2:7, 8a). The angels said to Lot, "Get out of here! Flee this place! The wrath of God is coming!" Lot and his daughters fled the city of Sodom and were spared (Genesis 19:12–27). For God had promised Abraham that He would not destroy the righteous with the wicked, and for the sake of ten righteous He would not destroy the whole place (Genesis 18:32). If there had been just ten righteous, God would have spared the city.

I believe that the influence of the church, as weak as it is, is the saving grace of America today; and if this influence, weak as it is, wasn't here, the judgment of God would have already fallen.

I'm convinced that one of these days very soon the Lord is going to remove His church. He is getting ready to say, "Come out of her, my people" (Revelation 18:4). "Then we which are alive and remain shall be caught up together with them in the clouds, to meet the Lord in the air" (1

Thessalonians 4:17). And God's judgment is going to fall again upon a godless, Christ-rejecting, blasphemous society.

What a paradox! People hate and curse the church, and yet if it wasn't for the influence of the church within their society, they would already have been destroyed. Jesus said, "Ye are the salt of the earth" (Matthew 5:13), "Ye are the light of the world" (Matthew 5:14). Your influence as a child of God is keeping back the wrath and judgment of God from being poured out even now upon our nation.

Again, it is interesting to follow Paul's comments on this subject in Romans 1;

> The wrath of God is revealed from heaven against all ungodliness and unrighteousness of men, who hold the truth in unrighteousness, ...[for] when they knew God, they glorified him not as God (Romans 1:18, 21).

You see, men became proud. They didn't give God the glory and the credit for what He had done, but "their foolish heart was darkened. Professing themselves to be wise, they became fools," and they began to glorify and serve the creature more than the Creator, who is blessed forever (Romans 1:21, 22, 25).

For this reason God gave them over to a mind that was void of God, and ultimately God gave them up to all kinds of vile practices including homosexuality and lesbianism.

Even as Paul recounts this, he speaks of the wrath of God which must come against this ungodliness and unrighteousness. We're living in the last days, and the judgment of God will soon fall. If it doesn't, God owes an apology to Sodom and Gomorrah—because we see the same sin here and its ultimate and final manifested form: open, aggressive homosexuality.

What a challenge and commission God has laid upon the church! "Ye are the salt of the earth" (Matthew 5:13). In those days, one of the chief uses of salt was as a preservative to prevent putrefaction of meat. They would salt the meat to kill the bacteria after they butchered it. Jesus said, "You're here to prevent the putrefaction." But this putrid world only tells us that we're not doing our job as we should.

God help us.

# CHAPTER 14

# WHERE ARE YOU?

Genesis is the book of beginnings. The word *Genesis* means "beginning." And thus, we have the beginning of the universe. "In the beginning God created the heaven and the earth" (Genesis 1:1).

Then we have the beginning of life forms, and the beginning of man. When we come to man, we find that he is vastly different than the other life forms God created. With the other life forms, God spoke and they existed. But God formed man out of the dust of the earth, so that man actually became God's handiwork. God may speak other creatures into existence, but there was a special molding and shaping of man by God, as He formed him after His likeness and in His image.

> And the LORD God formed man of the dust of the ground, and breathed into his nostrils the breath of life; and man became a living soul (Genesis 2:7).

There is a touch of God upon every man, even today. A definite distinction exists between the body that God formed out of the earth and the life that God imparted into that body, for man is really spirit. The spirit was formed when God breathed into that body the breath of life. The body is the dwelling place, the house, where the spirit of man lives. Created in the likeness of God, man was created with the capacity for fellowship with God.

There is something beautiful about the story in Genesis 3:8–9 where we read, "And they heard the voice of the Lord God walking in the garden in the cool of the day" (Genesis 3:8). God came down to commune with His creation. What a beautiful picture! But what a tragic picture as we continue to read,

> And Adam and his wife hid themselves from the presence of the Lord God...And the Lord God called unto Adam, and said unto him, Where art thou? (v. 9).

Why would Adam hide from the presence of God? It was neurotic behavior, because Adam possessed a guilty conscience. How futile for Adam to try to hide himself from the presence of God!

The psalmist David understood the futility of trying to hide from God.

> Whither shall I go from thy Spirit? Or whither shall I flee from thy presence? If I ascend up into heaven, thou art there: if I make my bed in hell, behold, thou art there. If I take the wings of the morning, and dwell in the uttermost parts of the sea; even there shall thy hand lead me, and thy right hand shall hold me (Psalm 139:7–10).

I can't escape from the presence of God. Yet whenever I feel guilty, a neurotic behavior pattern makes me think that I can hide my guilt from God.

Many people don't go to church simply because they have a guilty conscience. They figure that if they stay away from church they can hide from the presence of God, as though God dwelt in the church, as if you could just close your doors and pull the shades on God!

Paul the apostle said, "For in Him we live, and move, and have our being" (Acts 17:28). Job 12:10 says, "In whose hand is the soul of every living thing, and the breath of all mankind."

You might say the only way you can escape from God is to stop breathing, but even then you don't escape from Him. You'll enter into a clearer consciousness of His presence at that moment of death. There's no escaping from God! It's crazy to think that you can.

Psychologists today tell us that most neurotic behavior patterns stem from a guilt complex. It began with Adam. He felt a consciousness of his guilt, so he tried to hide from the presence of God. What caused the guilt complex? Adam disobeyed the command of God.

Looking at the overall story, God gave Adam the commandment for his own good and welfare. God knew the poison that was in the tree of the knowledge of good and evil. Adam was deceived into thinking that God was somehow trying to hold him back from a pleasant experience, that God didn't quite understand his real needs. Adam thought that by disobeying he could find a quality of life that God was withholding from him. But in reality, God knew what He was talking about. After Adam ate of that tree, he couldn't reverse his action. He couldn't go back and be innocent. To his dismay, he discovered that God was right all along!

There are men today who, like Adam, are deceived about the law of God. They look upon God's law as being very restrictive. "God's trying to hold back something good from me. He's trying to keep me from being happy." Men today are still willing to violate the law of God, thinking that they know better than God the needs of their own lives. But then they discover that once they've violated the law of God, it's irreversible—they can't go back and undo what they've done. They realize that God was right all the time. But now they have that sense of guilt, and they try to avoid God. Worse than that, they've lost fellowship or contact with God, and their lives become dead, empty, and purposeless.

God's purpose in coming into the Garden of Eden was to restore fellowship. When God came into the Garden, Adam hid himself. God cried, "Where are you?" That wasn't the call of an arresting officer, but the heartbroken cry of a loving father whose child had gone astray.

It's wrong to assume that man doesn't know the truth about himself. Deep down inside, each of us is aware of where we are. We spend much of our lives trying to conceal the truth we know about ourselves. We'd be embarrassed if other people knew what we know about ourselves. So, we create an image for others to behold; we want them to admire us, look up to us, think well of us. We do our best to cleverly disguise the truth we know about ourselves. Sometimes we're so clever in our own deceptions that we actually deceive ourselves.

The Bible speaks about those who have deceived themselves, and the truth is not in them (1 John 2:4). We actually begin to think, "Did God really say that? Well, God doesn't really care. Surely I can violate His laws, and it won't have any effect upon me. Surely I can escape the judgment of God." Man begins to deceive himself. But deep down inside he's not fooled.

Deep down inside we hear the Spirit of God crying out, "Where are you?" We try so hard to hide the truth, but the truth will win out. And though we may be successful in hiding the truth from other men, we cannot hide it from ourselves. The truth has its own way of working itself out—either in some form of emotional disturbance or in neurotic behavior patterns.

The Bible says, "All things are naked and opened unto the eyes of him with whom we have to do" (Hebrews 4:13). To think that I'm hiding from God is sheer folly. So, when God's cry comes to me today, "Where are you?" there are just two places I can be. I'm either in fellowship with Him, or I'm out of fellowship with Him.

God wants you to have full, rich fellowship with Him, because He knows the benefits that are yours by fellowshipping with Him. He wants you to share in His life and His glory. Instead of discarding Adam, God came to him and asked, "Where are you?" God doesn't forsake you and say, "Well, he had his chance." God comes to you and says, "Where are you?"—so that you might see yourself and evaluate yourself. As the Scripture said, "For if we would judge ourselves, we should not be judged" (1 Corinthians 11:31). Therefore, let each man examine himself.

"Where are you?" With Adam, his sin had created a breach. It separated him from God. So, we have the beginnings of sin and the beginning of man's alienation from God. Sin always alienates a man from God. Isaiah the prophet declared,

> Behold, the Lord's hand is not shortened,
> that it cannot save; neither his ear heavy, that
> it cannot hear: but your iniquities have

separated between you and your God (Isaiah
59:1–2).

The effect of sin in man's life is always broken
fellowship and alienation from God. Since God seeks to
restore you, He has made provision for your sins. That
which Adam lost in the Garden, that life and fellowship of
God, has been restored to you through faith in Jesus Christ.

"Where are you?" You know the answer better than
anybody else. But you don't have to remain where you are.
You can find forgiveness. God has made possible the
reversal of past actions. He has made the elimination of
past guilt possible. God has made such a total provision
for forgiveness that the past is removed as though it never
existed—in order that you might know the glory, blessing,
and joy of fellowship with God.

"Adam, where are you?" Where are you today? Are
you walking in harmony and in fellowship with God, or do
you find yourself alienated from that life of God?

A life that is out of fellowship with God is out of
harmony with its own nature, because God has created
you for fellowship. There is a natural restlessness in that
man who is apart from God. The Bible says,

> The wicked are like the troubled sea, when
> it cannot rest, whose waters cast up mire and
> dirt. There is no peace, saith my God, to the
> wicked (Isaiah 57:20–21).

Yet, rest for your soul is exactly what Jesus has
promised for you, if you would come to Him. He said,

> Take my yoke upon you, and learn of me; for I
> am meek and lowly in heart: and ye shall find
> rest unto your souls. For my yoke is easy, and my
> burden is light (Matthew 11:29–30).

Your mind is troubled by your life and the world around you. The turmoil that you see in our society has created the inner turmoil. "What's it all coming to? What should I do? How can I escape all these problems?"

There is a place of refuge, a place of strength, a place of fellowship with God. Though the worlds are moved around me, though the mountains be cast into the midst of the sea, I need not fear—because God is with me, His presence, His power, His love. He will protect, guide, and sustain me.

Are you walking in fellowship with God today, or are you trying to hide from God? If you're trying to hide from God, it's sheer folly! You're doomed to failure. You'll never hide from Him. Better that you open up your life and heart to God, and find the forgiveness of your sins and the restoring of fellowship with Him, for you and your family's sake.

# CHAPTER 15

# RETURN TO YOUR FIRST LOVE

> Nevertheless I have somewhat against thee, because thou hast left thy first love. Remember therefore from whence thou art fallen, and repent, and do the first works; or else I will come unto thee quickly, and will remove thy candlestick out of his place, except thou repent (Revelation 2:4–5).

The final messages of Jesus to His church are found in Revelation 2 and 3, as Jesus addresses Himself to the seven churches of Asia. Over and over as He addressed Himself to the things within the church, He exhorts, "He that hath an ear, let him hear what the Spirit saith unto the churches." Perhaps some of the most important things for the church to know and to understand today are these messages of Jesus to His church.

## Works

As we look at the church in Ephesus, we find that it had a lot of things going for it. Jesus, first of all, speaks of its works and labors. It was a church of bustling activity. A lot of works in the name of the Lord were being wrought in Ephesus.

Ephesus was, no doubt, a well-organized, well-functioning church. They probably had their witness teams, visitation teams, pulpit committees, church growth committees—and all of them were functioning well. The Ephesians were a model of organization and structure, but they had one big problem. Though they possessed a well-ordered machinery, God never wanted machines to do His work.

God never wants your work for Him to be mechanical. If God had wanted machines to do His work, He would have created machines to do His work. If God wanted your service to be mechanical, He would have created robots, and they could have done a better job than you're doing. God isn't interested in mechanical responses. God is interested in a loving response from your heart and from your life.

### Patience

The second characteristic of the church of Ephesus was its patience. Now, throughout the New Testament the churches had been exhorted towards patience, waiting upon the Lord to accomplish His work and to fulfill His promise.

Patience is certainly a desired virtue. How I wish I had more of it! How often I am impatient with the things of God. He isn't working quite as rapidly as I'd like Him to work, so I get in and try to help Him out, always with disastrous consequences.

Throughout the New Testament the church was exhorted towards patience in waiting for the coming of the

Lord. I wish the Lord would come soon. I look around, and I have to confess I'm excited; because I realize that the things happening in the world today could very well trigger the whole end-times finale. The worldwide economic system is becoming computerized. ID numbers will be tattooed on your wrist. Iran is falling apart and has taken an anti-Israel stand. The Soviet Union seems to be gearing up for a big move in the Middle East, with its takeover of Afghanistan. The whole thing is coming together!

I get impatient waiting for the Lord. "Lord, this is a great opportunity to return. You've got the whole thing lined up. Why don't You go for it?" And yet, the Lord has His perfect timing. James 5:7 said,

> Be patient therefore, brethren, unto the coming of the Lord. Behold, the husbandman waiteth for the precious fruit of the earth, and hath long patience for it, until the early and latter rain.

There is yet a harvest to be reaped for the Kingdom of God. He is waiting for it. All I need is patience, as He waits for His complete harvest. I often get so impatient with some of the stubborn-headed people who are holding things up. I wish you'd get on with it, so the Lord would get things over with!

## Purging

The church of Ephesus had patience, an admirable quality. Not only that, the church wouldn't tolerate evil persons. The Lord said of the church, "...how thou canst not bear them which are evil."

One of the great weaknesses of the church today is that the church so often will tolerate evil people just because they're wealthy. Churches are often seeking to win the favor of the rich, and they'll sometimes tolerate evil people who are rich, or they'll allow the evil ones to become part of the fellowship because they're famous. But there is always a weakening whenever evil or evil persons are tolerated within the church.

When a church body becomes so weak that it can no longer purge itself of the poisons in its system, that body will soon die. The church always needs to be strong. It needs to be able to purge the evil from its system, lest it die. The church of Ephesus had that quality. There was a certain purity there. They wouldn't tolerate those who were evil.

### Discernment

Finally, on the plus side, the Ephesians had a discerning spirit. The church could pick out those men who came along claiming apostleship, but were not apostles. The Ephesians wouldn't allow pretenders in the pulpit. John Todd would never have had a chance in Ephesus. (See *Christianity Today*, Feb. 2, 1979, for expose on Todd). He'd never have gotten in the pulpit there, because the church had a discerning spirit.

### Love

In spite of all of the good and positive aspects of the church, one negative aspect was so great that it nullified all the positives. The Lord said, "Nevertheless, in spite of all these positive factors, I have this against you—because you have left your first love."

You see, it is quite possible for a church to continue with all the motions, but be lacking in the chief emotion of the

Christian experience. We must be careful, because the Lord is far more interested in what motivates our activity than in the activity itself.

Jesus tells us to take heed to ourselves, examine ourselves, and be careful when we do our righteous deeds so that the motive isn't to be seen by men, to be a people-pleaser.

So often in our service for God we're concerned about what people might think of us. Sometimes we're motivated by the desire for people to know how talented we are. I'll sing for the Lord or play an instrument for the Lord, so that people will see how talented or how sweet and good I really am. I want people to think well of me. I'll do certain things for God, so people will think that I'm just a fine fellow.

Our motivations are often people-oriented rather than God-oriented. I should be far more concerned about what God thinks of what I do, rather than what people think of the things that I do.

Jesus gave us a good test in the Sermon on the Mount: What do I do when nobody's looking? Do I only pray when people are watching? Do I only give when it can be observed by others? If my motives are right, I'll be praying in secret and giving in secret. I'll be doing things for God without fanfare or bringing any attention to myself. I'll be serving the Lord just as easily and readily when nobody knows and nobody sees, because my motivation now is God-oriented. As Paul spoke of his own prayer life, "God bears me witness."

God wants only one motivating force in your life, and that is love. If you cannot and do not serve God because you love Him, then don't serve Him. If you don't give to

God because you love Him, then don't give. The last time the plate went by you, you may have thought, "I don't want the people in the pew to think I am a skinflint. So, I'll put something in." If that was your attitude, then for God's sake get your money back, because God doesn't want anything done for Him except out of the love of your heart for God. Whatever you do—whatever you give of service, time, or goods—if you aren't giving out of a heart filled with love, then don't give it at all. God doesn't want it. In fact, it's an insult to God.

Any time you go around moaning about what you've given up for God, what you've given to God, or what you're sacrificing for God, then you're insulting God. And He says, "Keep it! I don't want it!" He doesn't want you going around complaining about what He requires or demands of you. If you can't do it with a heart of love, it's much better that you don't do it at all, because you'll find yourself in the place of Ephesus. You'll be doing all kinds of work for God, but you won't have the right emotion. You'll be going on in works, but God won't recognize them. God doesn't even want them.

Paul the apostle said, "For the love of Christ constraineth us" (2 Corinthians 5:14). If your works don't come with God's constraining love in your heart, then surely you shouldn't be doing what you're doing, even if you're doing it in the name of Jesus. Anyone doing anything for the Lord must examine the motives of his own heart. "Why am I doing this?"

Paul said, "If we would judge ourselves, we should not be judged" (1 Corinthians 11:31). We're told that in the day of judgment our works are going to be tried by fire, to see what sort they are (1 Corinthians 3:13). What motivated me to do it? Unless the motivation was my love for Jesus, then the works that I've done will be burned. No credit, no reward.

This issue is so important that Jesus told the church that unless there were some immediate changes in Ephesus, He would come quickly and move the candlestick out of its place.

Now, what was the place of the candlestick?

> These things saith He that holdeth the seven stars in his right hand, who walketh in the midst of the seven golden candlesticks (Revelation 2:1).

The candlestick was in the presence of Jesus. Jesus is saying that though a church may do all kinds of works, may have great patience, may purge itself of evil, and be able to discern the false apostles—if they're not motivated by love, Jesus said, "I'm leaving."

The Lord isn't interested in all the hustle and bustle and activity of a church. He's interested in the love that comes forth. Only those works and gifts that are prompted by my love for Him will He accept at all. You may find many churches today with all kinds of social activities and concerns, worshipping in elaborate buildings with glorious choirs, and presenting tremendous lectures. But when you look around you won't see Jesus, except as He is depicted in the stained glass windows. The Lord has long departed their fellowship, and the people are worshipping in a tomb—cold, dead, religious forms, lacking the vitality of the love and life of Jesus Christ.

Jesus said, "Unless you turn, I'll leave. I'll not stay around, unless the love is there." God doesn't want anything from you apart from love. Love has to be the underlying motivating factor of whatever I do for God.

Jesus first wants me to give Him my love. Whatever else comes must come as a result and in response to the love that I have. Otherwise there is no value to it whatsoever.

## Remember

The call of Jesus to His church was first of all to remember from whence they had fallen. Remember the first love that you had for the Lord? Remember those days when you first found Jesus Christ as your Lord and Savior and realized that your sins had been washed away? Oh, how excited you were! You wanted to go out to the beach, out in the streets, everywhere to tell everybody about the love of Jesus. You were ready for any kind of a sacrifice and challenge, because the love of Christ was burning in your heart and soul. Jesus said, "Remember therefore from whence thou art fallen" (Revelation 2:5).

It's always a tragic and tell-tale sign of spiritual decay if you can remember a time in your life when you were closer to the Lord than you are today. It means that you're on the spiritual decline.

## Repent

"Remember therefore from whence thou art fallen, and repent" (Revelation 2:5). To repent means to turn. Turn away from your cold indifference, mechanical responses, dead works, and let your love for Him again fill your heart to overflowing. Fall in love with Jesus all over again!

He said, "Do the first works." Remember, repent, repeat. Go back to that first love, back to those first works prompted by love, back to that reckless and careless abandon for Jesus Christ. It doesn't make any difference what they say. It doesn't make any difference what it costs. Ah, just the opportunity to serve the Lord—and my love for Him burning within, driving me, pushing me into those sacrifices and labors of love.

Unless the love took first place in Ephesus, the Lord said, "I'm leaving." You may stick around in a loveless church, but He won't. He wants your love more than anything else. If you can't give Him that, don't give Him anything.

Maybe it's time to say, "O God, I'm sorry!" Repent! Turn and offer yourself again to serve the Lord. Maybe the serving you've been doing has become an old, stale routine. There's no life and joy in it anymore.

If your excitement and joy of serving the Lord has left, it's time to repent, time to go back to zero and start over. Return to your first love, that first excitement of relationship, that first overwhelming love and desire for Him. And may the things that you do for the Lord be prompted by a heart that is overflowing with love!

# CHAPTER 16

# THE SERPENT OF BRASS

*And Moses made a serpent of brass, and
put it upon a pole; and it came to pass,
that if a serpent had bitten any man,
when he beheld the serpent of brass,
he lived.*

And the people spake against God, and
against Moses, Wherefore have ye brought us
up out of Egypt to die in the wilderness? For
there is no bread, neither is there any water;
and our soul loatheth this light bread.

And the Lord sent fiery serpents among the
people, and they bit the people; and much
people of Israel died. Therefore the people
came to Moses, and said, "We have sinned, for
we have spoken against the Lord, and against
thee; pray unto the Lord, that He take away
the serpents from us." And Moses prayed for the
people.

And the Lord said unto Moses, "Make thee a fiery serpent, and set it upon a pole: and it shall come to pass, that every one that is bitten, when he looketh upon it, shall live."

And Moses made a serpent of brass, and put it upon a pole, and it came to pass that, if a serpent had bitten any man, when he beheld the serpent of brass, he lived (Numbers 21:5–9).

I am convinced that complaining is a state of mind. I believe that it is possible to have your mind set in a pattern of constant complaining, and that it can become a habit of your life and extremely difficult to break. Some people get to the place where they can see the bad in anything. It's just their mind-set, the way they think.

I may say, "You won the Irish Sweepstakes! They're going to give you $568,000!" Then they'll say, "Oh, that's horrible! Think of all the taxes I'll have to pay!" They can see something to complain about in every issue of life.

One of the prevailing sins of the people of Israel was their constant complaining. True, they did have something to gripe about. For 38 years their main dietary staple was manna. They had been eating this stuff for almost 40 years in the wilderness. It was a very bland food, just a little bit of sweetness and extremely mild (Exodus 16:31). No doubt it did become rather sickening after 38 years...breakfast, lunch, and dinner—manna. I can understand getting tired of it and saying how their souls loathed this light bread.

"We're sick of it. We're tired of it." So, Israel began to complain against the Lord and Moses. In reality there was much to be thankful for in this manna. If they didn't have the manna, they would have starved to death many years earlier. They should have looked at it and said, "Thank

God for the manna this morning! If it weren't here, think of how hungry we would get."

---

*Complaining is a state of mind. I'll say, "You won the Irish sweepstakes!" The complainer will say, "That's horrible. Think of all the taxes I'll have to pay!"*

---

Though there was something perhaps to gripe about, on the other hand there was plenty to be thankful for, as God did provide them with the manna to keep them from starvation. It was no doubt extremely nutritious. It had all they needed as far as vitamins and minerals to sustain their lives and keep them going. In fact, Psalm 78:24–25 says that this manna with which God fed them was actually angel's food. But even when you give some people angel's food, they can find something to gripe about.

---

*The people of Israel confessed, "We have sinned because we spoke against God and against you." They recognized that their complaining was actually a sin. The Word of God tells us to be thankful in everything.*

---

That seems to be true of every circumstance in our lives. No matter what happens to us, we can find something to gripe about; or no matter what happens to us, we can find something to be thankful for. Some people have that beautiful capacity of seeing something good in everything. No matter what has happened, they can accept it, they can flow with it and see some potential good in every situation. Some people can see potential danger or evil in every situation. It's how you have set your mind. Your mind can be set in a pattern of thanksgiving, or your mind can be set in a pattern of complaining. That becomes the pattern of your life itself.

One viewpoint says that no matter what happens, be thankful, be happy, and watch God work things out. The other believes that no matter what happens it's horrible, it's the end of the world, you're never going to make it beyond tomorrow, this is the end. Some people live in these crises all the time. They go from one to the next. Life is just one continual disaster, because that's the way they look at it. That's their mind frame and attitude. Expect the worst, then you'll never be disappointed.

What many people don't realize is that complaining is a sin. The fiery serpents came into the camp and began to bite the people, and they began to die. The people of Israel recognized this was a judgment of God because of their complaining. So, they came to Moses and said, "We have sinned because we spoke against God and against you." They recognized that their complaining was actually a sin and that God looked upon it as sin. The Word of God tells us to be thankful for everything. "In every thing give thanks: for this is the will of God in Christ Jesus concerning you" (1 Thessalonians 5:18). Since God has ordered you to be thankful, for you to complain is a sin.

Once each year in this country we celebrate Thanksgiving. We have set aside one day when we say "We need to be thankful." So, for one day we're thankful. I feel it would be much wiser if we would set aside a national Gripesgiving Day. One day each year we would air all of our gripes and complaints. Then the other 364 days we would be thankful. We'd go around thanking God for everything! Actually, we shouldn't even have a Gripesgiving Day because complaining is a sin.

---

*God gave a choice to the people.*
*"I'll provide the healing. But you're*
*going to have to do something about it*
*yourselves. You'll have to exercise your*
*power of choice."*

---

God brought judgment into the camp of Israel because of their complaining. Deadly snakes began to strike the people, and they began to die. So, the people came to Moses, confessed their sin, and said, "Pray for us."

It's interesting that when Moses prayed, God didn't just heal the people. He could have, but He didn't. Instead, He said to Moses,

> Make thee a fiery serpent and set it upon a pole: and it shall come to pass, that every one that is bitten, when he looketh upon it, he shall live (Numbers 21:8).

God gave a choice to the people. "I'll provide healing. I'll provide for your forgiveness. I'll provide for your living.

But you're going to have to do something about it yourselves. You're going to have to exercise your power of choice."

Moses made a serpent of brass. Brass is a symbol of judgment, and the serpent is a symbol of sin. "When you've been bitten by the snake and you're lying there dying, turn and look at the serpent on the pole. You'll be healed. You'll not die of the snake bite."

Imagine a man in convulsions lying on the ground. He has been bitten by one of these snakes, and he's dying. I run up to him and exclaim, "Hey, friend, look! Take a look in the center of the camp. There's a brass snake up on a pole. Just look at it and you'll be all right!"

He whines, "Don't give me that, man! I don't understand that at all. How can looking at a brass snake help me in this condition? Do you expect me to look at that when I don't understand it?"

"Hey," I reply, "I don't know how it works, but I know it does! I've seen hundreds of people all around you in the same condition. They were dying, too! But they looked and now they're all right! They're walking around in good shape."

"Yeah," he says, "but get a load of all those hypocrites who are looking. I don't want to look when there are so many hypocrites looking!"

I plead, "You're going to die if you don't look."

"Ah, don't bug me, man! Get off my case! I'll look when I'm good and ready." And the guy dies.

I say, "You fool. All you had to do was look and you would have lived. That wouldn't have been so difficult.

God didn't lay out some big trip. He made it so simple for you. You could have lived so easily. All you had to do was look at God's provision and you would have lived. But you have chosen death in your own folly, for whatever reasons."

God has looked upon man that way throughout time. God cried out through Ezekiel, "...turn ye, turn ye from your evil ways; for why will ye die?" (Ezekiel 33:11).

---

*As Moses lifted up the serpent in the wilderness, even so must the Son of man be lifted up: that whosoever believeth in Him should not perish, but have eternal life (John 3:14, 15).*

---

In the New Testament (John 3:1–15) Jesus confronted Nicodemus. Nicodemus came to the Lord at night and said to Him,

"We know you're a teacher that has come from God: for no one can do the things you do unless God is with him."

Then Jesus said to him, "Nicodemus, you've got to be born again."

"What are you talking about, Lord? Born again? I'm an old man. I can't go back to my mother's womb and be reborn."

"No, no, Nicodemus, you don't understand. That's a fleshly birth. Each man must also have a spiritual birth. For that which is born of the flesh is flesh; and that which is born of the Spirit is Spirit. Don't be surprised because I tell you that you've got to be born again."

Confused, Nicodemus asked, "How can these things be?"

> As Moses lifted up the serpent in the wilderness, even so must the Son of man be lifted up: that whosoever believeth in Him should not perish, but have eternal life.

That's the answer to the question of how a man can be born again.

Even as the brass serpent on the pole was a sign of God's judgment for their sin, our sins were all judged at the cross. Jesus bore the sins of the world at the cross. The Bible in Isaiah 53:6 says,

> All we like sheep have gone astray; we have turned every one to his own way, and the Lord hath laid on him the iniquity of us all.

So there at the cross Jesus Christ bore the judgment of God for all the sins of mankind.

---

*The word is nigh thee, even in thy mouth,*
*and in thy heart... That if thou shalt*
*confess with thy mouth the Lord Jesus,*
*and shalt believe in thine heart that God*
*hath raised Him from the dead, thou*
*shalt be saved.*

---

God is saying, "If you'll just look at my Son hanging there on the cross and believe that I have sent Him to bring you life, you can live, you can be healed, and you can be forgiven of your sins. Just by looking and believing." God has placed salvation within the reach of every man.

Paul said that salvation isn't something way up in heaven unattainable by us, where we have to say, "Who can go up there to bring it down to us?" Nor is it down in the depths so some guy has to "descend into the deep" and get it for you. But it is very close to every one of you. In fact, it's as close as your very mouth.

> The word is nigh thee, even in thy mouth, and in thy heart... That if thou shalt confess with thy mouth the Lord Jesus, and shalt believe in thine heart that God hath raised Him from the dead, thou shalt be saved (Romans 10:6–9).

But you have to exercise your capacity and power of choice by looking to the Lord Jesus Christ; and see in Him God's provision for your sin, for He bore the judgment that was due you for all your sins and transgressions. He died on the cross in your place, and as He died He bore the guilt of all your sins. That's why He died. If you'll just believe in Him and trust in Him, you'll be born again. Only then will you experience that glorious change in your nature.

---

*You may have your reasons for not looking*
*to Jesus Christ, but let me assure you,*
*they're all stupid. If you don't look,*
*you're going to die.*

---

There are some people who say, "Chuck, I'm a chronic complainer. I know I make people miserable around me. I wish I could look at the bright side of things, but I don't. That's just my nature." Yes, I agree, that's just your nature. But if anyone is in Christ he has a new nature. Old things are passed away and everything becomes new (2 Corinthians 5:17). That's what the Gospel is all about. God can change your nature from one of chronic complaining to one of continual thanksgiving. He can change you from what you are and make you what He wants you to be.

You may say, "Chuck, I would like to quit drinking. I know that it's destroying me, but I can't stop. I just have that kind of nature." Or you may say, "I don't like my horrible temper. I don't like what I do. I know it's destroying me and those around me, but that's my nature." Yes, that's your nature, but thank God your nature can be changed through the power of Jesus Christ. Just look to Jesus, and you can live.

---

*The person I feel sorry for and have little*
*hope for is the moral do-gooder. He*
*doesn't realize how dangerous his*
*condition really is.*

---

You know, I have great hopes for that person who recognizes his need. "Man, I know I'm guilty, but I've tried so hard. You don't know how hard I've tried, and I just can't do it. It's just not in me to do it." Such a man is close to salvation.

The person I feel sorry for and have little hope for is the moral do-gooder. The one who says, "I try to live by the golden rule. I do the best I can. I try not to hurt anybody. I always look at the positive side of everything. Really, I'm very satisfied with my life." That person is far from the kingdom. In fact, he is like a person in a euphoric state of mind who is freezing to death. "I'll just take a nap for a few moments, and then go on," but he doesn't realize how dangerous his condition really is.

This is the condemnation, that God sent light into the world, but men won't come to the light (John 3:19). It's the man who realizes that he is a sinner and in need of help and willing to turn to Jesus Christ who will be saved. In turning to Jesus Christ he finds the life and power of God infused into him, and he is changed. He knows and experiences that glorious power of God.

---

*Sin is the deadly malady that is destroying our world today. It's destroying humanity. It may be destroying you.*

---

You may have your reasons for not looking to Jesus Christ, but let me assure you that they're all stupid. If you don't look, you're going to die. If you will look, God's promise of eternal life is yours. You can be free from the guilt of your past sins. You can be innocent and pure before God. For "as Moses lifted up the serpent in the wilderness," even so was the Son of God lifted up, that whosoever would look and believe would be saved and not die.

Can any of you claim that you haven't been bitten by that deadly serpent of sin? Can any of you deny the presence of sin in your life? Romans 6:23 tells us, "...the wages of sin is death." Sin is the deadly malady that is destroying our world today. Take a look at what it's doing to people's lives. Look at the confusion and chaos in the world today. Why? Because of sin. It's destroying humanity. It may be destroying you.

There's only one provision that God has made—and that is through Jesus Christ, who took the judgment of God for man's sin upon Himself on the cross. He died in your place and provided for your salvation. Just look to Jesus Christ in faith and in trust, and you'll live forever with Him.

# CHAPTER 17

# GOD'S PLAN
# FOR THE AGES

The Bible says, "In the beginning God created the heaven and the earth" (Genesis 1:1). At some time after the initial creation, God created the angels who were assigned to various ranks. Some angels had higher positions than others, but all were under one government in the universe, the government of God.

## Satan's Rebellion

At some time deep in the past before God created the earth for man's existence, one of the high angels—called Lucifer, Satan, Dragon, Devil, Serpent—rebelled against the authority of God. Isaiah records this rebellion, which was an attempt by a created being to exalt himself above the Creator.

> For thou hast said in thine heart, I will ascend into heaven, I will exalt my throne above the stars of God: I will sit also upon the mount of the congregation... I will ascend above the heights of the clouds; I will be like the most High (Isaiah 14:13–14).

173

Satan's claim was, "I will, I will, I will." This exercise of his will against God's will was the rebellion in the kingdom of God.

For an unknown number of years until this point, beautiful harmony existed in the universe. Now another government came into being as Satan led a rebellion against this order of God and created within the universe a sub-government with himself in control. His is a government of death and darkness, against God's government of light and life.

### Man

The Book of Genesis declares,

> In the beginning God created the heaven and the earth. And the earth was without form, and void; and darkness was upon the face of the deep. And the Spirit of God moved [brooded] upon the face of the waters (Genesis 1:1–2).

In Genesis 1, God began His recreative acts, creating the earth and adapting it for man. When God had the earth ready, He "formed man of the dust of the ground, and breathed into his nostrils the breath of life; and man became a living soul" (Genesis 2:7).

When God created man and placed him upon the earth, He created him with his spirit uppermost. Man was spirit, soul, and body. Basically a spiritual being, man was created in fellowship with God within the government of light and life.

### Real Love

Had He so desired, God could have created robots. He could have created each one of us with a built-in mechanism that would automatically respond to certain impulses from God. God could project a particular impulse through the universe that would hit my brain, my arms would automatically go up, and I'd say, "I love You! Praise Your name!" Then my hands would go down.

However, could God really get love from an automatic response like that? How much love do you feel when you pull the string on a little toy doll that says, "I love you"? You know it's just an automatic response from a recorded message. You can't get much love from a mechanical object. You want a love from a freely-given response—and then the love is *meaningful*.

In order to have full fellowship with man and to receive real love from him, God created us as free moral agents. This means that man can do just what he pleases. No one is forcing him into a particular mold or response. Man is free to react and respond to God as he chooses.

### Environmental Conditioning

God created man, placed him on the earth, and surrounded him with every benefit and gift that would make for a happy, joyful life. God gave Adam a world full of pure water, clear skies, and abundant food. There was nothing around that would harm him.

A current philosophy claims that man's problems are due to his environment. All we have to do is improve a man's environment, and he can be changed from a slob into a prince. Improving the environment won't work with a pig. Change a pig's environment and what will he do? He'll be miserable until he gets back into the pigpen that he enjoys. Sociologically we can change a man's environment, but what happens? He's miserable until he gets back into the environment that he's used to.

By nature I'm a sinner. Change my environment by putting me around spiritual people and I'm miserable. "How long is that preacher going to talk? It's uncomfortable in this place! Why did I ever come here?" When the sinner gets around the moving of the Spirit, he becomes so unhappy. He's in a beautiful environment, but what does it do for him? It makes him nervous, upset, and fidgety!

Man's environment isn't his problem. Man's problem is his heart. That's where his sin lies. Man doesn't need a change of environment. He needs a change of heart. This can only be accomplished by the Spirit of God.

### Perfect Environment

Man was placed in the Garden of Eden in a perfect environment. He didn't have to work. God said, "There it is, Adam! It's all yours. Enjoy it! Have dominion over the fish of the sea, the fowls of the air, the beasts of the fields, and every living thing. I've made you the ruler. Be fruitful, multiply, and replenish the earth."

God also said,

> Adam, in this garden there is a tree that you're not to touch. You're not to eat of that tree. For in the day that thou eatest thereof thou shalt surely die (Genesis 2:17b).

The death process will set in.

We know that Adam messed up the whole thing, and God's curse came upon man and the earth. "Thorns also and thistles shall it bring forth to thee... In the sweat of thy face shalt thou eat bread" (Genesis 3:18a–19a). We know the result of man's failure in the Garden.

One day I was guiding a group of kids around Mt. Lemmon near Tucson. We had hiked up to the mining shaft and explored it. As we were hiking back down, one of the kids screamed out. He had brushed by an Ochoa cactus, commonly called the "jumping cactus," and it really clamped onto his wrist. I took a couple of sticks, carefully got them under the thorns of the cactus, and flipped the thing off his hand. As I was working to get the sticks underneath the thorns, this little kid was doing his best not to cry. He moaned, "That darn guy Adam!" I said, "You've had some good Bible teaching. You know where the thorns come from!"

Why did God put the forbidden tree in the Garden? Why didn't He just make a perfect environment without a tree to tempt man?

### Man and Woman

When God created man, He recognized that man by himself was incomplete. God said, "It is not good that the man should be alone" (Genesis 2:18a). God created the woman so that in her man might find fulfillment. There is the beautiful completeness that comes in marriage and is ordained by God. One day, after he had rebelled against God and created the government of death and darkness, Satan came to the woman who was in the Garden of God.

> And he said unto the woman, Yea, hath God said, Ye shall not eat of every tree of the garden? And the woman said unto the serpent,

We may eat of the fruit of the trees of the
garden: But of the fruit of the tree which is in
the midst of the garden, God hath said, Ye
shall not eat of it, neither shall ye touch it,
lest ye die (Genesis 3:1–3).

Satan replied, "Oh, you surely won't die! Don't you
realize that God is *afraid* that you might eat of that tree. He
knows that when you do, you'll be as smart as He is. He's
trying to protect Himself! You'll be amazed at how good
the fruit of that tree is! Why don't you give it a try? It'll
blow your mind" (Genesis 3:4–5).

### Two Questions

Two questions: First, why did God put the tree there?
Second, why did God leave Satan free?

The Bible says that ultimately a mighty angel will come
from heaven, take a chain, bind Satan, and cast him into
the abyss for a thousand years. After that Satan will be
loosed for a little while and then he'll be cast into Gehenna,
where he'll be out of commission forever (Revelation 20).

Since God will ultimately put Satan out of commission,
since God has the power to bind Satan and bottle him up,
why did God leave Satan loose in the beginning? Why
didn't He bottle up Satan from the start, so we wouldn't
have all these problems and troubles?

How beautiful it would be if there was no Devil! The
world and the flesh could be very beautiful if Satan wasn't
perverting it. The world is God's beautiful creation. "God
saw that it was good" (Genesis 1:25c). But Satan came
along and twisted, turned, and perverted it. We see our
fallen world and fallen flesh today. Why did God allow
Satan such freedom?

### The Test of Love

Why did God place the tree there? What did God want from man?

God wanted our love and fellowship. How could God know that we really loved Him and wanted to obey Him, if an alternative wasn't given? If there was no possible way to disobey or rebel against God, how could He know that we truly did love Him? How could God know how much we loved Him unless there was someone to exploit the alternative?

I could tell my son, "Stay in the backyard while I go to town. I need your help as soon as I get back, and I don't want to go looking for you." Then I take a big chain and bind him to the eucalyptus tree in the backyard. When I get home, my son is there, faithfully chained to the eucalyptus tree. I say, "Good boy!" I've got an obedient son, who did exactly what I told him to do.

My neighbor says, "You're only kidding yourself, Chuck. You should have heard all his screaming and cursing while you were gone. Your son was trying to break those chains!"

On the other hand, I could say, "Son, I'm going downtown now. Stay in the backyard so you'll be here when I get back." As I leave for town, I tell my neighbor, "Keep an eye on my boy, will you? I'm curious to see what he does when his dad's not around."

So I go and do my business, and my son's in the backyard. The gate is open. He's free. The kid from up the street comes over and says, "Hey, let's go to the school and shoot some baskets."

"No. My dad told me to stay in the backyard. I've got to wait for him. I'd like to go, but I can't."

"We can be back before your dad returns," the kid says. "We can watch for him, and as soon as we see him, we can beat him over and jump the fence. He'll never know you were gone. Come on, let's go!"

"No, my dad told me to stay here."

"Aw, you're chicken!"

"No, I'm not. My dad told me to stay here, and I'm going to stay here!"

So I get home and ask my neighbor, "How did it go?" He says, "You've got a good boy! Not only did he stay in the backyard, but the kid from up the street came over and did his best to talk him into leaving. Your son wouldn't follow his advice. He stayed right here the whole time. You can be proud of that boy!" I would be very proud. My son had every opportunity to go. Even the kid up the street tried to coax him, but my son remained obedient.

### The Fall

God has allowed man to be free. "You're free to enjoy the whole thing, Adam!" Satan comes along to exploit it. Imagine the joy God would have received if Eve had said, "Beat it, Satan! I wouldn't think of eating that. I'm going to obey God!" God would have surrounded Adam and Eve with His great love and showered it on them. Unfortunately, Eve believed the lie of the Devil. She was deceived, she ate, and all of a sudden her eyes were opened. She said, "Wow! Adam, give this a try!"

But Adam wasn't deceived. He knew exactly what he was doing, and he decided to join his wife. So he ate, and his eyes were opened. All of a sudden Adam and Eve realized right and wrong, the knowledge of good and evil.

Up to this point all they had known was good, obedience, and the love of God. But they had obeyed the suggestion of Satan, and now they knew disobedience, evil, and hate.

By taking of the forbidden tree, Adam and Eve acted in a double manner. They disobeyed God, but by the same act they obeyed Satan. They transferred their allegiance from God to Satan, from this government of God to this sub-government of death and darkness ruled by Satan.

### No Return

There was no way to scramble back. God had said, "For in the day that thou eatest thereof thou shalt surely die" (Genesis 2:17b). God's Word had to be fulfilled. God was bound to put them to death for their sin. He allowed the death processes to set in upon man, the breakdown within the cell structure known as the aging process. Man now lives under the government of death and darkness. He's alienated from God and finds himself with no way back.

### Hope in the Darkness

God could have obliterated His entire experiment when Adam disobeyed, but He didn't give up on man. God would show His supreme love to man and bring him forgiveness. God would take upon Himself a body of flesh, live among men, take the guilt and responsibility of man's disobedience upon Himself, and die for it. Man's sin would be punished.

### A New Nation

To accomplish His plan of hope, God needed a race of people through which His Son would be born. One day God spoke to a man in Babylon and said, "Abraham, I want you to leave this land of your fathers and go to a land that I will show you. I'll make you the father of a great nation, and out of your seed the Messiah, the Savior of the world, will come."

God guided this nation by sending it prophets who revealed God's plan more and more fully. They told where the Messiah would be born, the circumstances that would surround His birth, the miracles that would be accomplished, and the things He would do. In fact, the prophets foretold the very day that the Messiah would come to the nation.

Through the prophets God prepared this nation to look for their promised Savior. "When the fullness of the time was come" (Galatians 4:4), in God's perfect timing in the city of Bethlehem, there was born to a virgin a son. By instruction from the angel, the son was called Jehovah-Shuah, "God is salvation," for He was to save His people from their sins.

> [God] was made flesh, and dwelt among us (and we beheld his glory, the glory as of the only begotten of the Father), full of grace and truth (John 1:14).

John wrote,

> That which was from the beginning [with God], which we have heard, which we have seen with our eyes, which we have looked upon, and our hands have handled, of the Word of life (1 John 1:1).

> Who, being in the form of God, thought it not robbery to be equal with God: but made himself of no reputation, and took upon him the form of a servant, and was made in the likeness of men: and being found in fashion as a man, he

> humbled himself, and became obedient unto
> death, even the death of the cross. Wherefore
> God also hath highly exalted him
> (Philippians 2:6–9a).

So Jesus, Jehovah-Shuah, came as God promised. The prophet had declared,

> All we like sheep have gone astray; we
> have turned every one to his own way; and the
> LORD hath laid on Him [Jesus Christ] the
> iniquity of us all (Isaiah 53:6).

### The Open Door

Man exercised his own free choice in turning his life over to Satan and leaving the government of God. When Jesus Christ took the guilt of man's sin and died in his place, He opened the door so man could now leave this government of darkness and death and come back into God's government of light and life.

Even as man exercised his free choice to leave God's government for this other government, so must man exercise his power of free choice to come out of this government and return to God's government. By the tree of knowledge of good and evil man went from God's government to Satan's government. By another tree, the Cross of Christ, man can escape from Satan's control and return to God's government.

Again, it's a matter of free choice. God won't force you to obey Him or to serve Him at this point. A day will come when "...every knee shall bow... and that every tongue shall confess that Jesus Christ is Lord, to the glory of God the Father" (Philippians 2:10–11). For the present time, God is giving man the opportunity to exercise his free choice. If he wants to come into the fellowship with God, the way is now made open.

This government of Satan is like a circle. You may say, "I'm a very honest person. I believe in doing the best that I can and in living morally." Great! You're so good that you're at the top of the circle. Doesn't that make you feel good? But friend, you're still in that circle! As long as you're in that circle, you're in no better shape than those at the bottom who are crawling around in the mud.

### Purpose of Life

God is giving everyone the opportunity to come into fellowship with Him. This is the purpose of life. Man feels frustrated and empty until he comes again into fellowship with God.

I have an awareness that life should be higher and finer than what I have yet found it to be. I'm reaching out for something. Then I try this, but no, that's not it. So I try something else. And I'm on another desperate trip. I'm looking for something to satisfy my inner thirst to take away this frustration, and give me a sense of "Wow! This is what life is all about!"

But as long as I'm in the circle of death and darkness, there is no way that I can find the full meaning of life.

Why? Because in the beginning God created me for fellowship with Him. There will always be a void in my life until God comes in and fills it. God created me for His purposes, and I'll never be satisfied living for my own purposes.

Through Jesus Christ I can come back into fellowship with God. All I have to do is exercise my free choice and say, "Jesus, I take you as my Lord and Savior." The moment I do, I come through Jesus Christ into glorious fellowship with God, the King of light and life. Once again I can return to the beautiful sense of fulfillment, purpose, and meaning of life, because I'm walking in fellowship with God. This is what God created me for.

### His Return

Very soon Jesus Christ will come back to this earth and set up God's kingdom. Satan will be bound and cast into the abyss. For 1,000 years there will be a beautiful experience on the earth, as it is restored to its Eden-like glory and Christ reigns and rules over it. For a short season Satan will be released, but finally he'll be cast into Gehenna, the lake of fire burning with brimstone (Revelation 20:10). Satan will be forever out of the way, and there'll be only one government in the universe, God's government of light and life.

Everything within the universe will be in harmony and fellowship with God. God started out "in the beginning" with one government. It's going to end one day again with one government, all in obedience and subjection to God. The question is, "Where will you be at that time?" The answer lies with you.

If you choose the government of death and darkness, of rebellion against God's authority and Word, then that's where you'll be. The Bible says that Satan and all who follow him will be cast into the lake burning with "everlasting fire, prepared for the devil and his angels" (Matthew 25:41b; Revelation 20:10, 15). The lake of fire wasn't prepared for man. It was prepared for a rebellious Satan. However, those who have chosen Satan's government and rebel with him will be thrown into that place of outer darkness.

You have a free choice. God won't force you to love Him, serve Him, or come into His kingdom. That would be violating the whole principle of free choice. God wouldn't know whether you really did love Him. The only way God can know that you want to serve Him and love Him is by your voluntarily accepting Jesus Christ and choosing to come into His fellowship.

You're the one who decides your destiny. You can never blame God for what will happen to you or to any man. God has given us all a free choice. If you so desire, you can know His fellowship and His life. God has opened the way for you to have eternal life, but it's up to you to make your choice. What will it be?

# CHAPTER 18

# OUR GLORIOUS GOSPEL

When Jesus began His public ministry, He went into the synagogue in His hometown of Nazareth. He was handed the Scriptures. He turned to the Book of Isaiah and read this portion to them:

> The Spirit of the LORD God is upon me; because the Lord hath anointed me to preach good tidings unto the meek; he hath sent me to bind up the brokenhearted, to proclaim liberty to the captives, and the opening of the prison to them that are bound; to proclaim the acceptable year of the LORD (Isaiah 61:1–2a).

After reading it, Jesus closed the book and said, "This day is this Scripture fulfilled in your ears" (Luke 4:16–21).

Jesus closed the book after the reading, but Isaiah's prophecy doesn't stop there. Let's read on.

> And the day of vengeance of our God; to comfort all that mourn; to appoint unto them that mourn in Zion, to give unto them beauty for ashes, the oil of joy for mourning, the garment of praise for the spirit of heaviness; that they might be called Trees of righteousness, the

planting of the LORD, that He might be glorified (vv. 2b–3).

The glorious "good tidings" that we proclaim to you today is God's glorious message to man. In a world filled with so much misery, strife, and trouble, it's good to hear some good news for a change.

## Message for the Meek

Reading the newspapers or watching the news on TV gives a sad commentary on man's existence. Oh, how ready we are for some good news! The Gospel is good news, but who is it for?

In reading from Isaiah, Jesus declared, "The spirit of the Lord is upon me, because he hath anointed me to preach good tidings," the Gospel "unto the meek." The Gospel is for the meek, those who are conscious of their inadequacies and needs and are reaching out for help. The best way to understand the word "meek" is to separate it: me...ek. When I realize how "eeky" I am, I know what meek is all about. The Gospel is for those who recognize their need for something more, who are dissatisfied with their current status, who desire a better life.

Many people today are very satisfied with their lives. They're satisfied with their possessions and situations. The Gospel isn't for them. Other people today are extremely proud of themselves. The Gospel isn't for them, either.

## The Gospel Message

What does the Gospel do? First, it is meant "to bind up the brokenhearted." We've seen Valentine's Day cards that show broken hearts. Sometimes the heart is broken through the middle and sometimes it is totally fractured. Our hearts often break because of unreciprocated love. We have a deep love for another, but it's not received and accepted. This causes our hearts to break. I wonder how many times God's heart is broken over us.

Our hearts often break over our own failures and weaknesses. We promise ourselves that we'll do certain things, but we don't seem to be capable of achieving them. So, we experience heartbreak over our inadequacies. Our desire to be what we apparently can't be and to achieve what apparently is beyond our capacity causes personal heartbreak.

The Gospel has come to bind up the brokenhearted, to let us know that we can be what God would have us to be. The good news is that we can achieve, attain, and experience a love that flows and flows and doesn't quit. The second thing that the Gospel does is "to proclaim liberty to the captives." Paul spoke of those who had fallen in the snares of the Devil and had been taken captive by the Devil against their will (2 Timothy 2:26). Many people today have fallen into the snare of the Devil and have been taken captive by the Devil against their own will. In another passage Paul referred to those "who through fear of death were all their lifetime subject to bondage" (Hebrews 2:15).

We often use the term "free moral agent," but it's almost a misnomer. To say that a man is a free moral agent when he cannot help but do the things he does is a contradiction. If some compelling force is driving you to do things even when you don't want to do them, you're not free. You're a captive.

Sin often comes to you with a sugar-coated covering. You taste it and "Wow!" you plunge right into it. After the sugar is gone, you taste the bitter portion and try to spit it out. But now it's lodged in your throat and you can't get rid of it. If you're controlled by a cigarette habit or if you've got to have a drink, don't tell me you're a free moral agent. You're a captive—and the bitterness is just pouring into your system.

The Gospel of Jesus Christ has come to set free those who are captive. He can break every snare and deliver men from all the bondage of corruption that has held them in its power.

The third thing the Gospel does is "the opening of the prison to them that are bound." Today the Gospel will open the prison that you find yourself in.

When we were in Ecuador, the missionaries told us that if we get involved in a car accident, even if it's not our fault, the best thing to do is to go immediately to the airport and catch the next plane out of the country. When you're involved in an accident down there, guilty or innocent, you'll land in jail. You have to stay in jail until you can prove you're innocent, but you may not get a court date for five years. And in Ecuador they don't feed the prisoners. Someone on the outside has to feed you or you'll starve to death. And that's one of the nicer things about the jails.

I've also heard about the Mexican jails. If you get thrown in, your influence in the United States doesn't mean anything to the judge. They say the best thing is to stay out, because once you're in, you're really in. I don't know how true that is, but I don't want to experiment to find out.

Let's say that you're in jail in Mexico. You've tried every way to get out. You've written to the Mexican government, the American consulate, the UN. You've done everything, and you've finally concluded that you're not going to get out. So now you want to escape. Someone comes along and says, "I have a friend who can get you out."

"How can your friend get me out? Man, I've tried everything."

"He can."

"What makes you so sure?"

"He's freed thousands of others." "Really! What do I have to do?"

"Just trust him." "But how's he going to do it?"

"I don't know. He has his own ways, but I know he can."

"But if I don't know how he does it, I'm not sure I want to trust him."

"It's your choice, friend. Either rot in jail or take a chance."

We find ourselves in the prison of our own lust and sin. The good news comes that there's One who can deliver us, set us free, open the doors of the prison and liberate us. But we've got to put our trust in Him completely. We've got to commit ourselves totally into His hands, trusting that He can do what He has promised. We can be assured that He's already delivered thousands out of that same jail. He has set multitudes free from the bondage of sin. He can set you free today from your prison, if you'll give Him a chance.

There is an urgency in this Gospel of Jesus Christ, "...to proclaim the acceptable year of the Lord." Though the

Lord is offering you this freedom today, His offer is subject to withdrawal at any time. You see, Jesus Christ is under no obligation to save you at all. He doesn't owe you anything. His offer comes to you strictly because He is so good and loving that He hates to see you in a mess. So He offers to set you free.

However, this offer will be withdrawn—just when, we don't know. God told Noah, "My Spirit shall not always strive with man" (Genesis 6:3). If you reject His offer today, you can't be sure whether the offer will be good tomorrow. "Behold, now is the accepted time; behold, now is the day of salvation" (2 Corinthians 6:2). "Seek ye the LORD while he may be found, call ye upon him while he is near" (Isaiah 55:6). "Remember now thy Creator in the days of thy youth, while the evil days come not, nor the years draw nigh, when thou shalt say, I have no pleasure in them" (Ecclesiastes 12:1).

We proclaim to you "the acceptable year of the Lord." "Now is the accepted time." Now is the time for you to receive this glorious Gospel. Now is the time for you to be set free.

There is coming a "day of vengeance of our God" (Isaiah 61:2). His offer will then be withdrawn and men shall experience nothing but what they justly deserve for their sins: the "day of vengeance of our God."

### The Gospel Power

What will the Gospel do for you? Verse 3 reads: "to give unto them beauty for ashes" I love the *power* of the Gospel! I've seen the effects of the Gospel, and I've seen it bring beauty for ashes. Some people are burned-out, wasted, and destroyed. I've seen the Spirit of God take those burned-out lives and remake, remold, and reshape them into new and beautiful men and women.

I think of Mike MacIntosh, the pastor of our church in San Diego. When Mike first came to church, he was totally burned-out. He had taken so much acid and speed that he thought a bag was over his head and a .45 pistol was going off inside his brain. He would hear the explosion over and over. As I watched this handsome but totally burned-out young man, I wondered if he would ever recover from the damage done to his brain cells. I saw God take these ashes and begin to work with them—mold, shape, and change. I saw God restore Mike's wife and children. I saw God restore all that he had lost through his own folly.

Today, I see that beautiful young man standing before a glorious congregation in San Diego, with the glow of Jesus on his face and the love of Christ radiating from his life. I realize the power of the Gospel gives "beauty for ashes."

"The oil of joy for mourning" (Isaiah 61:3). Many people today find themselves in deep depression and sorrow of heart, grieved not only over themselves and their inadequacies, failures, and inabilities to cope, but with all of society. Our glorious Gospel gives "the oil of joy for mourning." It will lift your life from depression, sorrow, despair, and despondency to joy and hope.

The Gospel will also give you "the garment of praise for the spirit of heaviness" (Isaiah 61:3). Jesus said, "Come unto me, all ye that labor and are heavy laden..." (Matthew 11:28). If the burden you're carrying is heavier than you can bear, if you feel pressed down by life and by your circumstances, our glorious Gospel will fill your heart and life with praises unto God. How glorious to see people who once wallowed in the dejection and hopelessness of this world now walk with a spring in their steps, a smile on their faces, and the garment of praise covering their lives. That's the effect of this glorious Gospel.

### The Gospel Glory

What is the purpose of the Gospel? That we "might be called Trees of righteousness, the planting of the LORD, that he might be glorified" (Isaiah 61:3). God has done His work so that we might glorify Him. "To God be the glory, great things He hath done." As we see lives change—men and women set free and remade through the power of Jesus Christ, born again by the Spirit of God—we give glory to God for His work. These hopeless lives are now "Trees of righteousness, the planting of the LORD." The changes are God's work wrought in them, and there is no other explanation for it.

So often a man who has fought against alcoholism has been defeated by it. His life is burned-out, and he's now an outcast. You see him in the street in his pitiful condition. He has cried out for help. His family has tried to help him. But finally everyone has given up, and we call him a bum. As the power of the Gospel touches the ashes of his life and begins to turn him around, it changes and sets him free. The Gospel liberates him from that prison and makes of him a glorious person, beautiful to behold, a tower of strength within the community.

Only the Gospel can do that, and only God can be glorified for it. That's the purpose of the Gospel.

### The Gospel Truth

You ask, "Just what is the Gospel, the Good News?" Just this: Though you have failed and sinned, God loves you. God loves you so much that He sent His Son to set you free from your prison. If you'll put your trust completely in Him, He'll free you today, change your life, and make you what God wants you to be.

We have a glorious Gospel, but there's only one difficulty. To be effective it has to be applied. A fellow once asked a minister, "If your Gospel is so great, why isn't everyone a Christian?" The pastor responded, "If soap is so good, why isn't everyone clean?" Does the fact of dirty people testify against the value of soap? No. It works, but you have to apply it.

Have you?

# CHAPTER 19

# BURNING HEARTS

It was the first day of the week, the first day that people could travel home after the Sabbath holidays. Under Jewish law, two-thirds of a mile was the limit for Sabbath Day journeys and Emmaus was six miles from Jerusalem. Two men who were disciples of Jesus started off on the road to Emmaus, mourning over the tragic events that had transpired this particular Sabbath. They had just experienced the most bitter disappointment of their entire lives.

They had been disciples of Jesus for some time and life had been exciting and the future looked bright. How their hearts thrilled every time He touched a sick person and that person was healed. How their hearts thrilled every time one would cry out "I can see! I can see!" and they realized that He had opened blind eyes. They had seen Him raise the dead back to life. The joy and thrill of seeing the power of God demonstrated became overwhelming as they walked with Him, as they listened to Him and saw the works that He was doing. To these disciples came a growing conviction that indeed He was more than just a man.

They came to realize that He was the Son of God; that He was God's Messiah and that He was to be the Savior of the world. They realized that He came to bring man to God, to salvation and to life. As this hope grew, their hearts were burning with the anticipation of that day when He would exalt His position and His throne and He would begin to rule and reign on the earth.

This last week saw their anticipation and their dreams crumbling in ruins. Rather than seeing Him crowned King of Kings and Lord of Lords, they saw Him mockingly proclaimed King of the Jews with a crown of thorns crushed onto His head and His body hanging on the cross. Even then, they probably harbored the hope, deep in their hearts, that He would perform a dramatic, last-minute miracle and demonstrate His power before these people by coming down off the cross and showing that He had triumphed; that He could triumph over even these adverse circumstances.

There was no last-minute miracle, however. They watched in despair as the crowd mocked and jeered Him as He hung there. They watched until finally His body went limp and His head fell forward, His chin resting on his chest. He was dead. With His death something died inside of them. All dreams were shattered and all hope swept away as they saw that limp body taken down from the cross, placed in the tomb and locked in as the stone rolled over the entrance. It was finished, they thought. He could not be crowned King now.

The two disciples trudged along the road to Emmaus, talking of these things and trying to sort out the tragedy in their minds. They tried to make some sense of these events as their hearts were overcome with sadness and disappointment. Jesus joined them on this journey, but they were so overwhelmed with despair that they failed to recognize Him.

When He asked them what they were discussing that caused them so much grief, they responded in amazement, "How could you be unaware of the things which have happened in Jerusalem the past few days?" As though He didn't know, He said, "What things?" They told of what had happened to Jesus, saying He was mighty in deed and word in the sight of God and all the people (Luke 24:18–19).

They still believed He was a prophet of God. They could not deny the miracles they had observed firsthand, but no longer did they believe that He was the Messiah, the Savior. He was dead. They expressed their sorrow, declaring: "We hoped that in Him was the redemption of Israel." But the fire had gone out with His death and now their hope was dead and their hearts were filled with despair. Even the reports from the women concerning the empty tomb failed to rekindle their belief and their hope.

Jesus said, "Oh fools and slow of heart to believe all that the prophets have spoken." Beginning with Moses, He explained, from the Scriptures, everything concerning Him; how the Messiah would have to suffer and die and rise again and finally enter into His glory.

### The Cure for Unbelief

In these two disciples on the road to Emmaus, we see the tragic consequence of unbelief. Unbelief is a blinding thing. Unbelief can keep you from seeing what is right in front of you. Unbelief kept them from recognizing Jesus Christ, even though He was right there with them. Unbelief can keep you from the joy God has for you. These two disciples should have been skipping back to Emmaus, whistling and singing and praising God for the victories. But unbelief had them walking back in tears and sadness.

Jesus joined these two because something vital and important had gone out of their lives. The fire of passion and love had gone out and He wanted to rekindle it. He wanted to fan the embers into flame and to fill their hearts once again with excitement and joy. He wanted them burning with love, hope, and anticipation. So He taught them from the Scriptures, starting with Moses and the prophets.

How exciting it would be to have a copy of that sermon! Jesus probably began in Genesis when man disobeyed the command of God and ate the forbidden fruit, then tried to cover his awareness of his guilt by sewing fig leaves to cover himself, but God provided the skins of animals for his covering. God was showing even then that sin cannot be put away by man's works, but only by a blood sacrifice.

He no doubt reminded them about how Abraham promised his son Isaac, believing that God would provide Himself a sacrifice. Then He probably called to their attention that the crucifixion took place on Mt. Moriah, the same mountain where Abraham declared this prophecy.

He then may have reminded them of the reason for the celebration of the Passover that they had just been through, as he recalled the time when the children of Israel were in Egypt and were commanded to kill a lamb and put the blood on the doorpost so that the life of the firstborn might be saved. Even then God was drawing a picture in their minds and hearts that would be fully comprehended when He sent His Lamb to die; so that through the shed blood, those who believe in Him might have everlasting life.

Then He probably noted the various sacrifices under the Mosaic Law by which a man comes from a sinful state into fellowship with God, and showed how those sacrifices were all pointing to Jesus Christ, the one perfect sacrifice that would put away sins once and for all, making fellowship with God possible for all men, for all time.

Jesus must have pointed out the prophecies in Isaiah concerning the child that was to be born of the virgin—how the government would be upon His shoulders, and His name would be called Wonderful Counselor, the Mighty God, the Everlasting Father, the Prince of Peace—but this Prince of Peace would first be despised and rejected by men. He would be wounded for our transgressions and bruised for our iniquities, and the iniquities of the world would be borne by Him and He would be numbered with the transgressors in His death.

Jesus probably reminded them of the cry in Psalm 22, "My God, my God, why hast thou forsaken me," and then took them through that Psalm, pointing out the prophecy of the pierced hands and feet, the dividing of the garments among the soldiers, and the casting of lots for the vesture.

He probably pointed to Daniel's prophecy of the coming Messiah 483 years from the commandment to restore and rebuild Jerusalem, but that Daniel predicted by the Spirit that the Messiah would be cut off and receive nothing for Himself at that time.

In many other books such as Hosea, Joel, Amos, Obadiah, Jonah, Micah, Nahum, Habakkuk, indeed throughout the Scriptures, I am sure He showed them all the things they had failed to see. In Zechariah he must have shown them the passage, "Smite the Shepherd," and "They shall look upon me whom they have pierced," and pointed out how He had to suffer all of these things

(Zechariah 13:7; 12:10). God had declared it, but God declared also in Malachi that He was the Son of Righteousness which would rise with healing in His wings.

As they walked along, the words of Jesus were so exciting that the time passed rapidly. When they reached Emmaus it was getting dark and they invited Jesus in. As He took the bread and blessed it and as He broke the bread, their eyes were suddenly opened and they recognized Jesus. Perhaps they saw His pierced hands. With this recognition, He vanished, as His mission was accomplished. They exclaimed to each other, "Did not our heart burn within us, while He talked with us on the way?" (Luke 24:32). Their hearts were burning once again with that passion, with that love, with that desire to give all to Jesus Christ and to live completely for Him.

Burning hearts! I believe that is the supreme need of the church today. The church has become a marvelous organization. Today we have better programs than the church has ever had in its history, but what lacks in much of the church are hearts burning with a passionate love for Jesus Christ. The Word of God created that flame, that burning in the hearts of those disciples. Jesus took the Scriptures and opened up the truth to them, and the Word of God set hearts on fire for the Lord.

### Blessed Heartburn

Many of you today have broken hearts. You can't understand the circumstances of your life. Like the disciples on the road to Emmaus, you are confused. Your eyes are focused on those tragedies that beset you. It seems that everything is going to pieces around you and all you can see are your problems, your disappointments, your shattered dreams. Your heart has grown cold as you have begun to doubt the love of God. God is desiring to work in your heart and life today. He wants to work in you His eternal plan of love and grace. He wants to rekindle a fire in your heart, a blessed heartburn! Walking with Jesus Christ will give you a burning heart. Listening to the Word of God will give you a burning heart.

Jesus exhorted the men on the road to Emmaus about their hearts of unbelief. Unbelief is a choice as belief is a choice. You can choose to believe in Jesus or you can choose not to believe. You can pick out evidence in either direction. It is a choice. If you will choose to believe in Him today, all of the proof you ever need will be given to you and your heart will begin to burn with God's love. Listen to the Word of God and your heart will burn with passion!

One of the beautiful hymns of the church sums up the concept of the burning heart very well:

> Teach me to love Thee as Thine angels love,
>
> One holy passion filling all my frame;
>
> The baptism of the Heav'n descended dove,
>
> My heart an altar and Thy love the flame.

(From the song, Spirit of God, Descend upon my Heart... by Gorge Croly and Dredrick C. Atkinson).

# CHAPTER 20

# WHAT IS A CARNAL CHRISTIAN?

---

*The Bible categorizes every man in one of three categories: natural, spiritual and carnal. Everyone falls into one of the three categories. The natural man is bad news. He walks in darkness and is alienated from God. The spiritual man has been made alive by the Spirit of God and is controlled by Him.*

*The carnal Christian, however, has enough of the Lord to be saved, but not enough of the Lord to rest in that salvation. He has enough of Christ to be miserable in the world, but too much of the world to be happy in Christ.*

*That's a terrible place to be.*

---

I read about a farmer who had an apple tree on the border of his orchard. Half of the tree's branches hung on his side of the property and the other half hung over the fence. Each autumn as the young boys would start back to school, they would walk under that tree and see those apples. When the apples started to ripen, the boys would beat on that tree with their sticks trying to knock those apples down before the farmer could get them.

The farmer was also watching that tree, and when the fruit started to ripen, he would go out there and beat on that tree so he could get his apples down before the boys did. The farmer said that that tree on the border of his field was the most beaten tree in his whole orchard.

I see a lot of Christians around who are getting beaten from both sides. They are getting beaten by the world and beaten by the Spirit. That's carnal Christianity.

Man is always trying to put himself and others into various categories. People often ask, "What church do you belong to?" or "What denomination are you in?" They are trying to pin you down and categorize you.

God has only three categories for man—the natural, the carnal, and the spiritual. Paul tells us about these categories in his letter to the Corinthians.

> But the natural man receiveth not the things of the Spirit of God: for they are foolishness unto him: neither can he know them, because they are spiritually discerned (1 Corinthians 2:14).

Then Paul says,

> But he that is spiritual judgeth (the word "judgeth" in the Greek means "discerns" or

"understands") all things, yet he himself is judged of no man (not understood by any man). For who hath known the mind of the Lord, that he may instruct him?... But, Paul said, we have the mind of Christ (1 Corinthians 2:15–16).

Paul then said,

I, brethren, could not speak unto you as unto spiritual, but as unto carnal, even as unto babes in Christ. I have fed you with milk, and not with meat: for hitherto ye were not able to bear it, neither yet now are ye able. For ye are yet carnal: for whereas there is among you envying, and strife, and divisions, are ye not carnal, and walk as men? For while one saith I am of Paul; and another, I am of Apollos; are ye not carnal? (1 Corinthians 3:1–4).

The natural man, the spiritual man, the carnal man; which of these three categories best defines your condition today?

## The Natural Man

Paul first talks about the "natural man." This is the way man is born. This is the man whose mind and life are governed and ruled by his body appetites. "What shall we eat? What shall we drink? Where shall we go?" The desires of the body occupy the mind and life of a natural man.

Paul said,

You hath he [Jesus] quickened [made alive], who were dead in trespasses and sins; wherein in time past ye walked according to the course of this world, according to the prince of the power of the air, the spirit that now worketh

> in the children of disobedience: among whom
> also we all had our conversation [manner of
> life] in times past in the lusts of our flesh,
> fulfilling the desires of the flesh and of the
> mind; and were by nature the children of
> wrath, even as others (Ephesians 2:1–3).

Paul tells us that the natural man does not receive the things of the Spirit of God. Jesus said that when the Holy Spirit comes, "He will reprove the world of sin, and of righteousness, and of judgment" (John 16:8). But the natural man feels no conviction for his sins; he sees no need of righteousness; and he's not really concerned about the judgment to any great extent. If he were, he wouldn't be a natural man for very long!

The natural man doesn't feel the conviction of the Spirit of God upon his heart or within his life. He doesn't understand the love of God or see the need for redemption. He doesn't believe in Jesus Christ any more than he believes in any other prophet who might have lived. And he doesn't understand the Word of God: the Bible is a mystery to him.

Paul said that the natural man does not receive the things of the Spirit, for they are foolishness to him. The apostle said that "the preaching of the cross is to them that perish foolishness" (1 Corinthians 1:18).

The idea of Jesus Christ dying on the cross for man's sin is ridiculous to the natural man. The natural man believes that everyone has to make his own way: "Just do your own thing." The idea of Jesus taking his sin and guilt and then dying in his place is silly to the natural man.

When Paul was preaching before King Agrippa about Jesus Christ and His resurrection from the dead, Festus the Roman governor cried out, "Paul, your much learning has made you mad! You have been studying too hard (you've flipped!), talking about resurrection from the dead!" (Acts 26:24). The Gospel was foolishness to Festus. He couldn't receive the things of the Spirit.

Many times the natural man will pick up the Word of God and say, "I'll read the Bible to see what God has to say." But he can't receive it or understand it. He cannot comprehend God's truths. Neither can the natural man know them, Paul said, for he lacks those faculties by which God's truths are apprehended and appreciated. Not only does he not receive the things of the Spirit, the natural man simply *cannot know* the things of the Spirit.

We know that the blind man does not appreciate the beauties of a sunset and the deaf man does not appreciate the beauties of a symphony. Why? Because each lacks the faculties by which these things are appreciated. Likewise the natural man, lacking the spiritual faculty, cannot understand the things of the Spirit. So he passes them off as foolishness.

Until my spirit comes alive, I really cannot know spiritual truths. Until God makes them knowable to me, I really can't understand them. Thus, it is folly to try to argue a person into believing in Jesus Christ. I fear for that person who has been won by argument to a faith. If he can be brought to a faith by argument, he can also be taken away from that faith by argument.

Paul, whose heart had been opened to truth by the Spirit of God, said,

> When I came to you [I] came not with excellency of [man's] speech or of wisdom, ...that your faith should not [rest] in the wisdom of men, but in the power of God (1 Corinthians 2:1, 5).

A man becomes spiritual because of the operation of God's work within his life.

The things of God are foreign to the natural man. The Word of God is an enigma to him. He doesn't understand the things of the Spirit, neither can he know them, for they are spiritually discerned.

## The Spiritual Man

The second category that Paul gives us is the "spiritual man." The spiritual man is one whose spirit has come alive through faith in Jesus Christ. His mind and life are no longer governed by the flesh and the desires of the flesh, but they are now governed by the Spirit of God. The first thing Paul says about the spiritual man is that he understands all things. It is amazing how God's Spirit opens up our understanding to the things that were previously a mystery. Once we've accepted Jesus Christ, the Bible suddenly becomes a very interesting and understandable book.

A young man came to evangelist Dwight Moody one day and said, "Dr. Moody, if you answer ten of my questions, I will become a Christian."

"That sounds like a fair deal," Moody answered, "but let me make you an offer. Kneel down with me and accept Christ right now. Then bring your ten questions to me tomorrow morning and I guarantee that I'll answer them all."

The young man said, "Very well, I agree." He knelt down and asked Jesus Christ into his heart.

The next morning when the young man came into the office, Dr. Moody said, "Okay, I'm ready. Fire away!"

The young man said, "There's no need. God answered all my questions last night."

The spiritual man understands all things. The Spirit of God begins to open up our understanding to the things of God—and it is just beautiful to see the work of God's Spirit in giving us this understanding.

### To Know

One little epistle in the New Testament, 1 John, is more or less dedicated to knowing. John uses the verb "to know" 39 times in this short epistle's five chapters.

In the Greek there are two different words for the verb *to know*. One is *ginosko*, which means "to know by experience." The other word is *oida*, which means "to know by an intuitive kind of knowledge." The Book of 1 John is almost equally divided in its usage of *ginosko* and *oida* for "to know."

In the first case, there are things which we come to know by experience, such as the grace of God within our lives. We know the grace of God because we've experienced the grace of God. That we *ginosko*.

On the other hand, much of what we as Christians "know" is known intuitively by the work of the Holy Spirit within our hearts. It's oftentimes difficult to tell a person how we know a certain truth. We just know it. "But how do you know it?" Well, I don't know how I know it, I just know that I know it!

This intuitive knowledge, *oida*, covers many areas. Once I've received Jesus Christ and my heart has been opened by the Spirit, I simply know and understand so many things because God's Spirit begins to give me the understanding.

It's like turning on a light. All of a sudden, things are so clear. We see them plainly because God's Spirit has opened up this whole dimension of the spirit. The spiritual man understands all things, but Paul said that he is not understood by any man.

Once you become a spiritual man, you are an enigma to the natural man. Natural people can't figure you out. Because of this, you become a threat and a challenge to them. So they begin to probe. They try to figure out what makes you tick, and why your attitudes are so different from everyone else's.

These people can't understand how you can have so much joy. They assume that you just don't understand what's going on. If you really understood the circumstances then there would be no way that you could be so happy. They try to explain to you over and over again how terrible things really are. The fact that you still have such joy within your life really bugs them, and they can't understand the peace that you possess.

Eventually, the natural man assumes that you just don't care. If you really cared, you would be upset, you would be in turmoil, and you would be reacting. The natural man cannot understand the peace that you have in Jesus Christ. Nor can these people understand your forgiveness or your willingness to forgive. They urge you to assert your rights and "sue them!" But you just want to forgive—and that really troubles them! They can't get over the fact that you're not standing up and asserting yourself. They say, "People will push you down! You've got to learn to demand your own rights!"

Natural people can't understand why you're not worried or upset, and why you don't want to go out with them to the bars—because how in the world can you face these problems unless you brace yourself with a drink? They don't understand your changed life and your changed desires. "You mean you go to church during the week, too?" The fact that you enjoy going to church mystifies them.

The spiritual man understands all things, yet he is not understood by any man.

### The Carnal Christian

Paul said, "Brethren, I could not speak unto you as unto spiritual, but as unto carnal, even as unto babes in Christ." The "carnal Christian" is the man who has been awakened by the Spirit of God to his need of Jesus Christ and has received Jesus Christ into his life as his Savior—but he has never submitted his life to the Lordship of Jesus Christ. Thus, he is one who believes in Jesus Christ as his Savior but is still ruled by his flesh.

Paul said, "I could not speak to you as spiritual but as carnal, even as babes in Christ. I have fed you with milk and not with meat, for you have not been able to receive it before, neither are you able now."

The carnal Christian lives in an arrested state of spiritual development. He has never grown beyond the crib or beyond the bottle. He is still as he was 15 or 25 years ago when he first came to Jesus Christ—in the infancy state.

### Carnal Characteristic #1

Nothing is more exciting than to have a baby and to see him grow and develop. You watch the baby as he first learns to coordinate and respond—those first responsive smiles are so exciting and beautiful. You see him discover his hands and body and watch him as he begins to walk. You hear him as he tries to communicate by sounds until he grows and matures and develops. Observing a baby's growth is a very beautiful and rewarding experience.

I thank God for the privilege of being a parent and watching my children grow up through those developmental stages. It was the most exciting experience that I could ever imagine.

I'll never forget when our first daughter said her very first word. I had been repeating "Daddy, Daddy, Daddy" to her over and over again. I was determined that her first word was going to be "Daddy." Every day I would smile and go through my routine with her.

One Sunday evening I was going into the closet for my suit coat and from the crib I heard it—"Daddy." I was shocked. I jumped. I yelled. I ran to the crib. "What did you say? What did you say?" I shouted. My baby daughter gave me the biggest, knowingest grin I had ever seen. I said, "Say it again! Say it again!" But she wouldn't. She just grinned.

I urged her to repeat it and when I turned to walk back into the closet, I heard it again. "Daddy!" I turned around to her big grin. I grabbed her, I squeezed her, I hugged her. Oh, what a time Daddy had with his little girl!

Now the years have gone by. If I were to walk into the room and see my same daughter still in a crib, and she'd look up grinning and say "Daddy!" then the experience wouldn't be joyful and exciting. It would cut like a knife in my heart. She should have developed. She should have grown. She should have matured. Infancy, when it's time to be an infant, is beautiful. But infancy, when the time has come for you to be an adult, is monstrous.

When we first come to Jesus Christ and offer our initial prayers to God, those early prayers are not very polished or smooth. Yet, I am certain that the Father's heart jumps with joy and excitement as we offer our first prayers unto Him. But, if after 20 years of arrested spiritual development we are still saying, "Now I lay me down to sleep, I pray the Lord my soul to keep…" then I am certain that it must hurt the heart of the Father.

Paul is saying that you haven't been able to take meat before nor are you now able to receive anything more than gruel. You've never developed enough to take meat. You've never grown beyond infancy. There is no depth of spiritual comprehension. You love the sermons filled with jokes and personal testimony because you're not able to feed upon the Word of God. You seek whatever amuses you. Lacking spiritual depth, you become more experience-oriented in your relationship to God.

### Carnal Characteristic #2

Another characteristic of the carnal Christian is that of striving—loving to get involved in situations to stir things up. The carnal Christian is a fault-finder. If he can't find a fault, then he will create a fault.

I was reading a sociological study of one of the subculture tribes in New Guinea. The sociologists were interested in this particular group of people because the tribe was always getting into huge fights. Every morning, before these people would get to the day's business, there was a big brawl.

The sociologists tried to figure out why the natives needed to fight each day. In studying the tribe, they found that its diet was very deficient. The people were living on the borderline of starvation and suffering from malnutrition.

The sociologists theorized that the tribesmen, so weak from their poor diet, could get enough energy for the day only by getting into a big fight and stimulating their adrenaline flow. Once their adrenaline started pumping, they had the energy to get up and do other things. The fighting was directly related to their poor diet.

It's interesting that Paul also relates poor diet and fighting to the spiritual life. Paul said, "You're not able to take meat. Thus, there are jealousies, strife, and divisions among you."

A poor spiritual diet will lead to strife. Because you need something to get you motivated, you get into arguments and situations that get you excited and stirred up. Then when you're good and mad, you search the Scriptures. But you only do it to prove your argument, not to really study and learn about God.

"So," Paul said, "there are jealousies among you." Jealousy always leads to division. Carnal Christians want to get everybody on their side, "Don't you think I'm right about this?" and thus they create divisions within the body of Christ.

Paul points out that some say, "I'm of Paul," while others say, "I'm of Apollos." He asked, "Isn't that carnal?" But what's the difference between saying that or saying, "I'm a Baptist," "I'm a Presbyterian," "I'm a Methodist," "I'm a Catholic"? I have found that the more spiritual a person becomes, the less denominational he is. We should realize that we're all part of the body of Christ and that there aren't any real divisions in the body. We're all one.

What a glorious day when we discover that God loves the Baptists!—and the Presbyterians, and the Methodists, and the Catholics. We're all His and we all belong to Him. We see the whole body of Christ, and we begin to strive together rather than striving against one another. But, as long as a person is filled with a haughty spirit, he will show the mark of carnality rather than real spiritual growth and maturity.

### Is a "Carnal Christian" a Christian?

Some people become very carnal as they challenge the phrase "carnal Christianity," arguing that the words are mutually exclusive. "If you're carnal then you can't be a Christian, and if you're a Christian then you can't be carnal." But Paul refers to them as both "carnal" and as "babes in Christ." They are in Christ—yet tragically they are still babes.

We are encouraged in many places in the New Testament to grow up. The word "perfect" in the Bible means "of full age, maturity." We are encouraged toward perfection, toward growing up, developing, and becoming mature in our relationship with God. Why? So that we might come into,

> ...the measure of the stature of the fullness of Christ (into that complete or fully matured man in Him): that we henceforth be no more children, tossed to and fro, and carried about with every wind of doctrine, by the sleight of men, and cunning craftiness, whereby they lie in wait to deceive; but speaking the truth in love, may grow up into him in all things, which is the head, even Christ (Ephesians 4:13–15).

May God help us to get beyond the infancy stage. Let's not be satisfied with the fact that we've received Jesus as our Savior, but press on until Jesus becomes the Lord of our lives and we become truly spiritual people—walking in the Spirit, led by the Spirit, and governed by the Spirit of God within our lives.

### Rest

In the Old Testament we have a beautiful picture of the children of Israel as they came out from the bondage of Egypt, passed through the wilderness, and ultimately entered into the Promised Land. "Egypt" represents the world and the "wilderness" represents carnal Christianity.

True, they're not in Egypt anymore. Praise the Lord for that. It's better to be a babe in Christ than to be a full-grown adult outside of Christ. Yet, they haven't entered into all that God has for them.

The Promised Land is a beautiful land of abundance, a land in which to settle down and make homes, a place to live off the land and share in the glory of God's promises. But we see the children of Israel in the unsettled condition of the wilderness as they're roaming around with no place to abide or to rest. Carnal Christianity is the unsettled condition of moving from place to place and never being rooted or grounded. For the carnal Christian there are no permanent victories. He can never claim an area or territory and say, "This is mine. I have conquered it."

> Let us therefore fear, lest, a promise being left us of entering into his rest, any of you should seem to come short of it (God has left us a promise of rest)...There remaineth therefore a rest to the people of God. For he that is entered into his rest, he also hath ceased from

> his own works (from his own strivings, from his
> own carnality), ...Let us labor therefore to enter
> into that rest (of God) (Hebrews 4:1, 9–11).

Pray to God that we will enter into the rest today and begin to grow so that we can take the meat of the Word, develop, and become truly spiritual.

In the parable of the seed falling on various soils, there was the seed that fell among thorns. The thorns grew up, choked it out, and that seed did not bear fruit. Jesus said that the deceitfulness of riches and the cares of this life are the thorns that grow up and choke out the fruitfulness in the Christian life.

Carnal Christians are like trees without fruit. Their lives never produce anything that is really beneficial to others. The life of a carnal Christian is barren, he is like a cloud without rain. You may say that there is some value to a cloud even if it has no rain. Yes, it casts a dark shadow wherever it goes. I've met Christians like that. They never bring any refreshing and reviving rain—only dark shadows. May God help us to avoid being ruled by our flesh and living as carnal Christians, so that we can walk in the Spirit totally and completely.

### Fence-Sitting

In the annals of American history there was a political group known as the Mugwumps. They were the fence-sitters. They were always trying to please both sides, so theirs was a miserable lot.

I never did find out why they were called Mugwumps, except that their "mug" was on one side of the fence and their "wumps" were on the other. A fence sitter is in a precarious position because he never fully satisfies either side.

You can never be fully satisfied as a carnal Christian. It's only as you give your life, your body, your mind, and your soul to the Lord and commit it all to Him, that you will know the joy, peace, and blessings of walking in the Spirit and being a "spiritual man."

*Maybe you would like to talk to the Lord about your own particular category. The Lord would like to talk to you!*

# CHAPTER 21

# STRANGE FIRE

When the children of Israel were in the wilderness, God gave Moses the design for the tabernacle, a place where people would meet God. God then anointed certain men among the Israelites with special building skills so that they could build the tabernacle according to the blueprint that God had given Moses on Mt. Sinai. They carved out the acacia boards and overlaid them with gold. They set them in sockets of silver and put the staves into the rings by the sides of the ark. They sewed the linen curtains, and they carved the cherubim over the top of the mercy seat. They laid on the goat's hair coverings, the red-dyed ram's skins, and then over all of those, the badger skins. When the brass altar was put in the front of the tabernacle with the brass laver, Moses and Aaron initiated this place where the people would gather to meet.

Beginning in Leviticus 9:22, we read of the dedication of the tabernacle:

> And Aaron lifted up his hand toward the people, and blessed them, and came down from offering of the sin offering, and the burnt offering, and peace offerings. And Moses and Aaron went into the tabernacle of the

congregation, and came out, and blessed the people: and the glory of the LORD appeared unto all the people. And there came a fire out from before the LORD, and consumed upon the alter the burnt offering and the fat: which when all the people saw, they shouted, and fell on their faces. And Nadab and Abihu, the sons of Aaron, took either of them his censer, and put fire therein, and put incense thereon, and offered strange fire before the LORD, which he commanded them not. And there went out fire from the LORD, and devoured them, and they died before the LORD. Then Moses said unto Aaron, This is it that the LORD spake, saying, I will be sanctified in them that come nigh Me, and before all the people I will be glorified (Leviticus 9:22–10:3).

From this passage of Scripture we know that as Moses and Aaron initiated the tabernacle according to God's plan; they cut the sacrifice of the burnt offering and laid it upon the altar and went in to offer the blood before the Lord. As they came out to the people, God's glory suddenly appeared and a fire from God came and kindled the altar and the sacrifice that was there. When the people saw this fire spontaneously begin to consume the sacrifice, they shouted and fell on their faces worshipping God. At this moment the two sons of Aaron; Nadab and Abihu, took some strange fire and put it in their small golden censers with incense. They rushed to offer it unto the Lord and as they did, fire came from God and killed them.

Why did God disrupt such an exciting occasion with the killing of Aaron's sons? All the people were filled with religious fervor and excitement, rejoicing and praising God. Suddenly God hushed them all as the fire killed the two boys and a fear enveloped the entire group. Why did God dampen the zeal of the people at that precise moment?

It is important for us to realize that what is said of God in the New Testament is also true of God in the Old Testament. In the New Testament we read "For God so loved the world" (John 3:16). God has always loved the world. God has always desired that all men should know Him. To demonstrate His love to the entire world, He chose the nation Israel and gave His law to its people. These were the laws by which a man might live in harmony with God and by living in harmony with God, might then experience the blessing, power, and presence of God in his life. Through the nation Israel, God wanted to demonstrate His love for the whole world and the advantages that people could have if they would fellowship with God and walk with Him by keeping His commandments.

Having chosen Israel to be His instrument, He then chose the tribe of Levi as His priests to be special representatives to the people. As the priest went in before God with an offering or sacrifice, he was a representative to God for the people. The priest was also God's representative to His people. In turn, the people were to be God's representatives to the world so that all people would know that God loved them.

God needed to keep a proper image of Himself before the people. If a priest misrepresented God or was evil in any way, the people and the witness of God would be corrupted. God wanted the world to know the truth about Him so that people would be drawn to Him. But here, as the priests were beginning their ministry, there was a failure among the sons of Aaron to properly represent God. This is why God dealt with them severely and immediately; to keep the people of Israel from getting a corrupt idea of God, and to save the rest of the world from a corrupt witness.

My heart breaks as I think of how often God has been misrepresented by His servants. I never stand before the church without the awesome consciousness that I am there as God's representative. I know it is important that I properly represent God so that people have a true concept of Him. If a situation arises and I react with anger or irritability when God isn't irritated or angered, I misrepresent Him to others. I am responsible to God for my misrepresentation of Him. I am constantly aware of the awesome obligation of every child of God to be His representative to the world.

As we read the story of Aaron's sons, we ask ourselves why they were slain. When we get to the 16th chapter of Leviticus, in the first verses, God speaks of the occasion of the death of Nadab and Abihu. Verse 12 says that God instructed Aaron to take the fire from the altar and put it in the incense. In other words, the fire for the incense offered to God was to come from the fire that God had kindled. But Aaron's sons had grabbed strange fire to offer to the Lord. They offered fire other than that which the Lord kindled and thus their work.

God doesn't want us to bring strange fire to Him. It is always important for us to examine our motives. Ask yourself just what is it that is motivating you to do this service or work for God. If there is any *fire* (enthusiasm or excitement) that is motivating you other than the fire that God has kindled in your heart, your service for God cannot be accepted. It is of no value. Therefore, we must examine ourselves and remember that the Scripture says if we will judge ourselves, we won't be judged of God.

A day is coming when our works will be judged by fire. God will see what motivations really were behind the things that we did for Him. Jesus said, "Take heed that you do not your [charitable deeds] before men, to be seen of them" (Matthew 6:1). If I were ministering only because it satisfied my psychological need for acceptance from people, then God help me! I would be serving Him with strange fire. If my motivation is to draw attention to myself and receive praise from men, then I am serving God with a false motive and it is unacceptable to Him. Paul said, "For the love of Christ constraineth us" (2 Corinthians 5:14). That burning love of Christ within my heart is the only true motivation for any service that I offer unto God. Good works have to come from a heart that is burning with the love of Jesus Christ.

A lot of strange fire is being offered to God today. Churches and para-church organizations are using all kinds of motivational gimmicks to get people to give, to support their ministries and thus serve God. Prior to leaving the denomination I had served for many years, I went to a conference in Phoenix, Arizona. The bishop stood before the ministers and declared to them, "I realize that motivating people by competition is carnal motivation but we must face the fact that most of the people we minister to are carnal and thus we need to motivate them with carnal motivation." My opposition to his statement was obvious, so I was invited for a cup of coffee with the bishop immediately after the service.

He began to talk to me about rebellion and I explained to him what bothered me about what he had said. I also felt that motivating people with competition was carnal, but how much better it would have been if he had said, "Let's seek to correct this by ministering to the people in a way that will make them spiritual people." If he had said that, I could have wholeheartedly agreed with him. But to suggest that because the people are carnal, pastors should come down to their level and use carnal motivation was wrong in my eyes. It could make it impossible to ever lead them to become spiritual people.

I told him I desired to be spiritual and I desired that my people be more spiritual. I didn't stay with the denomination very long after that and I'm glad, because I don't want to motivate people with carnal motivations anymore. I spent too many years in the ministry trying to push programs and trying to entice people to do the work of God with carnal motivation. I've given away too many giant beach balls, lollipops, bicycles, and who knows what else in an effort to generate enthusiasm in people for doing the work of God. I am tired of pushing people. I came to a place in the ministry where I said, "God, I'm so tired I can't push anymore programs; I quit." And I left the ministry, weary of offering false fire to God.

Then God began to kindle His fire within my heart. I felt that burning love for Jesus Christ and wanted to minister to people in the Spirit and let God do the work in their hearts. It is so beautifully easy when God does it!

Leviticus 10:9 gives us another hint of what went wrong with the two sons of Aaron. The Lord said to Aaron when his sons were killed,

> Do not drink wine nor strong drink, thou, nor
> thy sons with thee, when ye go into the
> tabernacle of the congregation, lest ye die.

It could be that Aaron's sons were drunk. In a half-drunken stupor, perhaps they really were not aware of what they were doing. As they sat there enjoying the dedication, the fire of God suddenly came and lit the altar.

Everybody was shouting with excitement and worshipping. In the excitement they grabbed their censers and put the coals and the incense in them and went in to offer this incense before God with an unclear mind because they were under the influence of false stimulants.

God doesn't want any service from false stimulation. He wants you to know what you are doing when you commit yourself to Him. He wants you to have a clear understanding of what that means. He wants your mind to be clear and sharp when you worship Him and He wants to know your actions are coming from a clear mind and a willing heart.

There is one more indication in the text of what possibly went wrong with the two boys. That is in verse three:

> And Moses said unto Aaron, this is it that
> the LORD spake, saying, I will be sanctified in
> them that come nigh me and before all the
> people I will be glorified.

You see, God doesn't want anybody seeking glory for themselves as they serve Him. It could be that when all of this excitement arose and all the people were worshipping God, that the sons of Aaron suddenly distracted people from what God was doing and drew the attention of the people to themselves by stepping out and offering their incense at an inappropriate time. At a time when people's hearts and attention were centered on God and God was ministering to His people, these two men with their false offering were an interruption. They sought only to glorify themselves by reminding the people that they were God's priests. God does not want anything or anybody to distract attention from Him. God will not share His glory with any man!

I realize that I have the awesome responsibility of properly representing God to you so that you don't get a false concept of God. I pray that you will also recognize your responsibility, because you represent God to the world and you can't let people get the wrong concept of Him. In everything you do for God, take care that your motivations are pure and that it is only God's fire that you are offering unto the Lord—and not the fire of your own enthusiasm or your personality. Make sure you have a clear mind and full knowledge of what you are doing. Make sure you have a willing heart and that you do your service to Him in a way that won't distract from the One that we have come to represent. Make sure that you don't take attention from God and call it to yourself, but that people see Christ through you.

May God help you be a true and faithful representative. God loves the world and He wants the world to know that. He has chosen you as His instrument. And you can walk in fellowship with Him and He can bless your life so completely that you will be filled with His joy, His power, and His love and the needy world around you will see the benefits of walking in fellowship with God.

# CHAPTER 22

# WHY GOD CRIPPLES

> And Jacob was left alone; and there wrestled
> a man with him until the breaking of the day.
> And when he saw that he prevailed not
> against him, he touched the hollow of his
> thigh; and the [socket] of Jacob's [hip] was out
> of joint, as he wrestled with him. And he said,
> Let me go, for the day breaketh. And he said, I
> will not let thee go, except thou bless me. And
> he said unto him, What is thy name? And he
> said, Jacob. [In Hebrew, Jacob means "Heel-
> catcher."] And he said, Thy name shall be
> called no more Jacob, but Israel: [Israel means
> "governed by God" in Hebrew] for as a prince
> hast thou power with God and with man, and
> hast prevailed (Genesis 32:24–28).

I believe God is in control of my life, and therefore,
nothing happens to me by accident. I believe that God rules
the affairs of my life; each thing that takes place has been
ordained by God. I also believe that God loves me
supremely. Believing these things often creates problems in
my mind. There are times when I have very painful
experiences and I'm hurt or sorrowed. I have difficulty
reconciling the fact that God controls my life and loves me
supremely with the pain that I sometimes go through. "If

God loves me," I reason, "then why is He allowing this to happen to me?" I think that I wouldn't inflict pain on someone I love. Why is God allowing me to suffer?

But that really isn't true, for in looking back I can see that I have often hurt those I love. I remember, for instance, that when our children were growing up, the boys would often run into the street without looking in both directions for oncoming cars. After repeatedly reminding them to be cautious when they crossed the street, I finally had to spank them for dashing into the street without looking first. Now why did I inflict pain on those little guys I loved so much?

Because I knew that if they didn't learn not to run into the street, they might really be hurt. To spare them the tremendous pain and suffering of being hit by a car, I deliberately inflicted a lighter pain on them.

In the story of Jacob, God not only inflicts pain, but actually cripples a man He loves. People often ask why God allows a person to be permanently crippled. In order to fully understand this, we need to take a closer look at Jacob's story.

Look first at Jacob himself. His name means *Heel-catcher* in Hebrew. He was the second-born of a set of twins. Because he took hold of his brother's heel just after he emerged from the womb, his parents called him "Heel-catcher." This later came to mean *supplanter*, or "one who overtakes someone by catching his heel." And that, surely, was the story of Jacob's life.

He was a shrewd, cunning man who had no qualms about cleverly taking advantage of any situation. Jacob was the kind of fellow no one liked to do business with, because he always managed to give everyone else the short end of any deal. If he met someone in the desert, dehydrated and dying of thirst, he was the type of person who would be happy to give him a drink from his canteen...for a price, of course!

Look at his relationship with his older brother Esau, who had the birthright. Jacob wanted his brother's birthright and watched for an opportunity to get it. He waited until a day when his brother Esau had been out hunting, and had come home famished and weary. Jacob was cooking a stew and Esau smelled the delicious aroma of the stew and asked Jacob to give some of it to him. Jacob said that he could certainly have a bowl of stew, if he would trade his birthright for it. Esau was hungry and tired and so he agreed to trade his birthright for just a bowl of stew. That's the kind of person Jacob was: a supplanter. He took full advantage of his brother's weakened condition and got the birthright in an unfair trade.

Jacob finally fled his home, fearing Esau's wrath for taking the birthright and the blessing away from him. He traveled to the home of his uncle Laban in Haran. He fell in love with his cousin Rachel and wanted to marry her but he lacked the money for a dowry. When Laban asked Jacob what he'd like to receive as wages for his labor, Jacob offered to work for seven years to earn the chance to marry Rachel. Uncle Laban okayed this plan, and it seemed that Jacob was finally settling down, and turning from his devious, scheming ways.

But Jacob had not counted on the craftiness of Laban, who proved to be just as conniving as Jacob had ever been. Jacob worked diligently for the seven years of their agreement. The day of the wedding came and there was a great feast of celebration that lasted far into the night. It was dark when Jacob went to his tent, saw his veiled bride, and consummated his marriage. In the morning, when he turned to gaze at his beautiful wife Rachel, he saw that Laban had substituted Leah, Rachel's older, ugly sister in her place. Jacob stormed from the tent and questioned his uncle, angrily demanding to know what had happened. He had served for Rachel and received Leah, and he was very upset. His uncle explained that the custom of the land dictated that a younger sister cannot marry until her older sister is wed. He told Jacob to work for another seven years, then he could marry Rachel too.

Jacob served the next seven years, married Rachel and stayed on with Laban because the uncle found that God had blessed him with Jacob's services. They established a regular wage for Jacob, but within about six years, Jacob had gained greater and stronger flocks than his uncle.

Laban's sons were furious, and, fearing again for his life, Jacob fled with his wives, children and servants. When Laban had discovered that Jacob was gone, he pursued him for seven days. The night before he reached Jacob, God spoke to Laban and warned him not to harm Jacob in any way (Genesis 31:24).

When Laban overtook Jacob the next day he told him of God's warning not to "speak good or evil" to him. Jacob then rebuked his uncle, saying that Laban would have sent him away with nothing if God had not intervened. They set up a pile of stones. Laban told Jacob not to cross over those stones to pursue him. Laban said "mizpah" and they parted. Now we have come to use this word as a pleasant benediction or good-bye. Something like: "May the Lord watch over thee while we are absent from each other." That's not what it meant to Laban. In the context here, it was more like "You're a dirty rotten thief. I won't be able to keep an eye on you anymore, so may God watch you and keep you straight." Laban wanted Jacob to know that God would be watching him, to keep him from behaving so underhandedly in the future.

The pile of stones they set up meant that Jacob couldn't go back to Haran, so he moved on and made camp at Manahaim. Jacob sent messengers ahead to let his brother Esau know he was coming home after a thirty year absence and that he possessed wealth, servants and cattle because God had been good to him. The messengers returned with the news that Esau was coming to meet him with an army of 400 men. Jacob knew his life was in danger because Esau vowed to kill him before he fled from home. Since he'd severed his relationship with his uncle, he couldn't go back past the pile of stones. He had no place to go.

When there's nowhere to turn, most of us look upward to God. That's what Jacob did, offering one of the most beautiful prayers in the Bible. (A prayer that is an excellent model for personal prayer.) As soon as he finished praying, he called his servants in and gathered 200 goats, and 20 he-goats, 200 ewes and 20 rams, 30 milk camels, 40 cows, 10 bulls, 20 female donkeys, and 10 foals. He set the animals into three herds, with a servant leading each herd. He sent the first group out, ordering his servant to drive them toward Esau and let him know that the animals were Jacob's gift to him. The other two servants were to do the same. Jacob set this up so that if Esau was angry, the servants were to give him their herds to appease him. The moment his brother softened toward him, Jacob ordered the servants to stop giving the gifts. Jacob was hoping the scheme would calm Esau's anger and save his own life. Though he'd just prayed to the Lord of help, he immediately returned to his manipulative nature.

After he made the arrangements with the servants, he took his wives and children across a brook near his camp and set them up for the night. He decided that he needed a good night's sleep to prepare for whatever the next day would bring, so he crossed back over the brook and bedded down alone, anxiously anticipating the confrontation he would have the next day with his brother.

As he lay there, the angel of the Lord came to him. They began to wrestle, and continued to struggle all night. I have done a little wrestling, and I know that just 15 or 20 minutes can really be tiring. Imagine wrestling all night with the Lord! In the morning, when Jacob still would not surrender, God touched his hip, shriveling one of his muscles, and causing his hip to lock permanently out of joint. It was extremely painful and tremendously crippling. Then the Lord told Jacob to give up because the day was dawning. Crying, Jacob refused to let go unless the Lord blessed him.

Then the Lord asked, "What is your name?"

Jacob replied, "Heel-catcher."

The Lord proclaimed, "Your name will no longer be 'heel-catcher,' but Israel [governed by God] for you have struggled with God and have prevailed" (Genesis 32:25–29).

How did Jacob prevail with the Lord? He was crippled in the struggle, so he must have lost the fight. But Jacob did prevail! Not by might, but through tears and prayer. That's how we always prevail with the Lord: through prayer, through weeping, through defeat.

Jacob was a conniver and a schemer. God loved Jacob and wanted to do many wonderful things through his life. God wanted to bless him beyond measure and use him to father the twelve tribes that would comprise the nation of Israel, from which He would ultimately bring His Son, the Messiah, into the world. God had marvelous plans for Jacob, but because Jacob was able to scheme his way out of every situation, God could not carry out those plans. It was Jacob's self-sufficiency that blocked what God wanted to do. God needed to break Jacob and bring him to the point where He could use him.

To accomplish this, God first brought the confrontation with Laban. The pile of stones was set up so that Jacob could not pass over them. Jacob was worried about Esau's army of 400 men coming toward him so he turned to God in prayer. But he immediately tried to figure out a way to appease Esau on his own, with the gifts of livestock. He was right back to his old tricks, planning, as a last resort, to flee if his brother was still mad enough to attack him. So the Lord wrestled with him all night, but Jacob still refused to surrender, so the Lord finally crippled him, taking away his option of running away from Esau. Then he could turn only to the Lord in his frustration and despair.

To properly understand the text that declares that Jacob wrestled with God and prevailed, we must read the commentary on this passage in Hosea 12:4. We read there that Jacob wept and sought favor from Him.

How did Jacob prevail against God? Through prayer, weeping and finally, through surrender. He triumphed when he came to the end of himself, saying, in effect, "I can't go any further. This is it, I've had it!" That was when he asked God for help. At last God brought Jacob to the place where He could fulfill His plans through him.

Why did God have to cripple Jacob? Because Jacob was so stubborn God had to break him before he would surrender himself to God's will. But it doesn't always have to be this way. If Jacob had surrendered during the struggle or if he'd just asked the Lord to help him, then the Lord would not have had to take such drastic measures.

Jacob was not the only one who refused to give in to the Lord. Look at Jonah. Did he have to spend three miserable days and nights in the belly of a whale, where, by his own description, he thought he was in hell? It was hot and humid and waves washed over him as he hovered in that disgusting, smelly place. Did Jonah have to go through all that? No! If he'd headed straight to Ninevah when God sent him, he would've never met the whale. It was only because he fled in the opposite direction that he learned that those who observe lying vanities are only making difficulties for themselves.

Many people, like Jacob and Jonah, think they can run from God or hide from Him. If you think you can do everything on your own, you're only making it tough on yourself. True victory comes only through surrender.

Maybe you're wrestling with God. And maybe you've just about come to the end. Perhaps God has touched you and crippled you in some way, or you're very close to that point. You've been fighting with God and you won't give in. You're still manipulating, you're still scheming and thinking, "...maybe if I just do this or that, then..." Perhaps God has to cripple you so that you'll realize that you cannot make it on your own. Then you would have to cry out to God for help. That cry of despair and hopelessness will really be the beginning of a glorious work of God in your life as He takes over and begins to bring about His plan of victory for you.

We prevail when we surrender totally to God. That's what happened to Jacob. It took a crippling injury to bring him to that point of surrender. I pray that you will not be so obdurate that God will have to cripple you to accomplish His purposes of love in your life.

We really misunderstand God and His ways most of the time. He loves you so much that He will keep you from doing things that might be life-threatening. He will not spare you pain if it is necessary to bring you to the point of total surrender to Him. That's exactly what God desires from you now, so that He can work out His plan for your life and do all the things He wants to do for you because He loves you so much.

Are you getting in His way? Your cleverness and self-sufficiency could be postponing the glorious work God intends to do through you.

I can picture Jacob limping as he crosses the brook back to his family. I can see Leah and Rachel running out and asking him what happened and why he was struggling so. I can hear him tell them not to call him "Jacob" (heel-catcher) anymore, but to call him "Israel" (governed by God) instead. That was his victory: his life once governed by his flesh was turned over to God. There will be victory in your life when you allow yourself to be governed by God, too. True victory comes when we surrender to Him.

# CHAPTER 23

# THE MORE SURE WORD

Today you sit in the judgment seat. You must make a decision concerning Jesus Christ. Is He the Son of God, or is He a shrewd charlatan? As a judge you must carefully weigh all of the evidence presented.

Often, an eyewitness report is the most powerful testimony. Peter declared he was an eyewitness of Jesus Christ:

> For we have not followed cunningly devised fables, when we made known unto you the power and coming of our Lord Jesus Christ, but were eyewitnesses of his majesty. For he received from God the Father honor and glory, when there came such a voice to him from the excellent glory, This is my beloved Son, in whom I am well pleased. And this voice which came from heaven we heard, when we were with him in the holy mount. We have also a more sure word of prophecy; whereunto ye do well that ye take heed, as unto a light that shineth in a dark place, until the day dawn, and the day star arise in your hearts: Knowing this first, that no prophecy of the scripture is of any private interpretation. For the prophecy

came not in old time by the will of man: but
holy men of God spake as they were moved by
the Holy Ghost (2 Peter 1:16–21).

The New Testament, for the most part, was written by
eyewitnesses of Jesus Christ's healing power. They wrote
of the works He did: healing the lame, the deaf and the
dumb, opening the eyes of the blind, straightening crooked
backs and even bringing the dead back to life. They also
witnessed His power over nature. They watched as He
turned water into wine, walked on water, and controlled
the elements with just His word, calming raging winds and
the waves of the sea with a command. They bore witness
to His death and resurrection from the dead; and wrote of
how He visited with them for some 40 days after His
resurrection, teaching them about the power and the glory
of God.

### They Bore Witness

As a judge, you must determine whether Peter and the
others are competent witnesses. Are their statements
reliable? Someone said: "You can't really believe their
witness; most of them were fishermen, and you know what
liars fishermen are!" However, it is interesting that one of
these fishermen recorded his own account of how he and
the others fished all night but caught nothing. He didn't
even try to tell about "the one that got away," but frankly
confesses the futility of their efforts.

Perhaps the whole thing was a big scheme. Suppose
they got together, sat down and carefully rehearsed their
story. They could have repeated it over and over again to
one another and questioned and examined each other until
they were sure they all had the same story. Then they
could have gone out and told their carefully concocted tale.

But Peter said, "We have not followed cunningly devised fables when we made known unto you the power and the coming of our Lord Jesus Christ, but were eyewitnesses of his majesty." He denied any hint of collusion and declared that their story was true. He made it known that he was an eyewitness; that he heard God's voice confirming what they had come to believe: that Jesus was indeed the Messiah, the Savior of the world, the Son of the living God.

Now if all of this was just an elaborately concocted fable, would all of them have died defending its truth? At least one of them would have broken under the strain of the threat of death. In fact, even Satan declared: "Skin for skin, yea, all that a man hath will he give for his life" (Job 2:4). His philosophy was that a man would give everything he had to protect his life, because life itself was the most important thing. If this is really true, then one of the "eyewitnesses" would have cracked under the strain, confessed the hoax and saved himself from tortures such as being crucified upside down or being dragged through the streets or being stoned or beaten. One of them, at least, would have tried to save himself. But all of them (with the exception of John, who died a natural death) were killed for the story they held to be true. They died because they declared that Jesus was the Messiah, the Son of God, and was indeed risen from the dead. The tremendous personal risk they took to spread their story makes theirs a powerful testimony.

### The Law of Compound Probability

Although Peter was one of the eyewitnesses, he does not ask that we believe only his testimony. He says that we should examine evidence even stronger than eyewitness accounts. He says we have "the more sure word of prophecy" (2 Peter 1:19).

For over a thousand years, holy, godly men wrote down the inspirations that God sent to their hearts, telling of One whom God would send to be the Savior of the world. They listed His birthplace, the circumstances of His birth, and the events of His life. They even predicted how He would suffer and the way He would die. Finally, they wrote of His resurrection.

Examining the records of these holy men of God, we find over 300 stipulations concerning the Messiah and what He would accomplish in His birth, life, death, and resurrection. It is fair to ask about the possibility of one person fulfilling all of the requirements by just "being in the right place at the right time." There is a way to compute the chance factor of this occurring.

The scientific "Law of Compound Probabilities" allows us to accurately calculate the chance of any prophesied event taking place. Each stipulation added to the prediction lessens the chance of the event's occurrence, because the possibility of several details coinciding is more remote than the possibility of one event occurring alone. When 300 details are considered, the chance factor becomes astronomical. Let's look at the Law of Compound Probability by starting with just eight of the biblical prophecies pertaining to the Messiah and calculating the possibility of one man fulfilling all eight of those requirements.

For instance, Micah 5:2 said Christ would be born in the city of Bethlehem. The chance of an individual being born in Bethlehem is easy to determine by taking the average population of Bethlehem since the time of the prophecy in about 725 B.C.—it turns out to be about 7,000—and comparing it with the average population of the earth—about 700 million. Divide the second by the first, and you find there is one chance in 100,000 of being born in Bethlehem.

Then Malachi 3:1 said there would be a forerunner who would go before Christ to prepare His way. How many men have had a forerunner prepare the hearts of the people to receive them? Though I can't think of any, let's say one in 1,000. Zechariah 9:9 said Christ would make His triumphant entry into Jerusalem on a donkey. How many of the great rulers of history have made their triumphant entries on donkeys? I don't know of any others, but let's say one in 1,000 again, to keep it conservative. Most triumphant entries are made on something like a majestic stallion or in a great chariot— certainly not on donkeys. But Zechariah said, "Behold, thy King cometh unto thee: he is just, and having salvation; lowly, and riding upon an ass, and upon a colt the foal of an ass." Zechariah also said He would be betrayed for thirty pieces of silver by a friend (Zechariah 11:12). How many men in history have been betrayed by a friend for exactly thirty pieces of silver? Again, keeping our estimates low, let's say one in 10,000.

Then Zechariah 11:13 added that the thirty pieces of silver would be used to buy a potter's field. What are the chances of that coincidence? Let's say one in 100,000, though I don't know of any others in history. Isaiah 53:7 says that, although He was innocent, He would make no defense. How many innocent men refuse to answer in their own defense when brought before a court? An innocent man falsely accused wants everyone to know about his innocence—that's a natural reaction. Still conservative, we'll say only one man in 10,000 would be silent in the face of false charges. Finally, Psalm 22 said that both His hands and feet would be pierced. On the average, how many men could you find with both hands and feet pierced? We'll say one in 10,000.

Multiplying these chance factors according to the Law of Compound Probability, we establish how many men we would have to look at before we found one who met all eight stipulations. The number of men would be 10 to the twenty-eighth power, or 10 followed by 28 zeroes. And ours were just conservative estimates! (We can subtract the total estimated population factor of 10 to the eleventh power, but that still makes the chance factor one in 10 to the seventeenth power.)

If you had that many silver dollars, you could cover the entire state of Texas with a layer of silver dollars two feet thick—and Texas is a big state! If you marked one of these silver dollars and let someone roam through them blindfolded, his chance of coming up with that marked silver dollar would be the same as the chance of one person just happening to fulfill the eight requirements laid out in the prophecies we looked at. But there were over 300 stipulations contained in the prophecies! Let's examine the chance of 16 requirements being fulfilled by one man.

Assuming the chance factors for another eight prophecies would be fairly equal to the factors of the prophecies we examined, there would be one in 10 to the forty-fifth power, or 10 followed by 45 zeroes. This is a number so vast that if you had this many silver dollars, you could make a ball of silver dollars with a diameter which would be 30 times the distance from the Earth to the Sun. Can you imagine marking one of these silver dollars and letting some fellow dive into the pile blindfolded? Can you imagine him grabbing the dollar you marked, just by chance? The coincidence of this is the same as the chance of Jesus fulfilling 16 of the prophetic requirements, just by accident. And again, remember, He fulfilled over 300!

Increase the number to 48 requirements. Now the chance factor increases to one in 10 followed by 157 zeroes, a number so huge our minds can't really conceive it. There's no way to make a ball this size of silver dollars. Even if there were enough silver dollars to make it, the universe is just too small. Let's compare the number to one of the smallest things we know—an electron. If two and a half quintillion electrons were placed single file, the line of them would only be an inch long. That would be 2.5 x 10 to the fifteenth power. To count these electrons would take one person nineteen million years of counting day and night at the rate of 250 per minute. Imagine how many electrons there are in a one inch cube—two and a half quintillion times two and a half quintillion times two and a half quintillion. To count that many would take 6,859,000,000,000,000,000,000 years!

Ten to the one hundred and fifty-seventh power electrons make a solid ball the estimated size of our universe, which has a radius of approximately six billion light years. In fact, if you could go into mass production and somehow start manufacturing these balls at the rate of about five hundred per minute, you could go on making them for six billion years (the estimated amount of time that this universe has been in existence) and you could do that 100,000,000,000 times over. Now if you marked just one of the electrons you had used to make the balls and asked someone to find it, the chance that it would be found by random selection is the same chance that Jesus had of fulfilling forty-eight of the requirements set forth in prophecy just by accident. And Christ fulfilled over three hundred!

That is why Peter said: I was an eyewitness; I saw it all happen; I heard it all. But if you don't believe me, look at something more sure than what I've seen and heard: evidence that is stronger than an eyewitness account. Look at the evidence of God's sure word of prophecy fulfilled by Jesus Christ.

### It's Time for Your Verdict!

In the prophecies mentioned, I didn't include Daniel 9:25, in which Daniel said: "from the going forth of the commandment to restore and to build Jerusalem unto the Messiah the Prince, shall be [sixty-nine sevens]..." (or 483 years). Because Daniel was computing with the Babylonian calendar, we refer to a year with just 360 days, so it was 173,880 days from the time of the commandment to restore and rebuild Jerusalem to the coming of the Messiah, according to Daniel's prophecy. Artaxerxes, the Persian king, was the one to command the restoration of Jerusalem in the year 445 B.C. on March 14. We know this because the Persian record has been preserved by God so we can be sure of the exact date.

Starting then, on March 14, 445 B.C. and marking the next 173,880 days off the calendar, we come to April 6, 32 A.D. This happened to be a Sunday, the day that Jesus made His triumphant entry into the city of Jerusalem.

Luke 19:41 tells us that Jesus wept over Jerusalem that day as He beheld it. Now how many men made a triumphant entry into the city of Jerusalem that day? Just one man, the one who fulfilled this and all of the other prophecies concerning the Messiah...Jesus Christ!

Now you must make your decision based on the evidence set out for you. Jesus asked, "What think ye of

Christ? Whose son is he?" (Matthew 22:42). Now you must answer that important question.

If your verdict is: "Yes, Jesus is the Christ, the promised Messiah," then you should make Him the Lord of your life. There is something very interesting about your decision concerning Jesus Christ. Though you are the judge, what you conclude will not change HIS destiny at all. Your decision determines your destiny because you will eventually be judged by your decision concerning Jesus Christ. He is what He is, whether you believe it or not.

John said, "And this is the record, that God hath given to us eternal life, and this life is in his Son. He that hath the Son hath life; and he that hath not the Son of God hath not life" (1 John 5:11–12).

It's time for your verdict. You have examined the evidence. What will you do with Jesus who is called the Christ?

*May the Lord bless you and may His love fill your heart and life to overflowing. What a joy and blessing for us to share with you God's Word and God's love!*